For Jenniffer and Evan

BURNING THE FURNITURE

by
Dan Smith

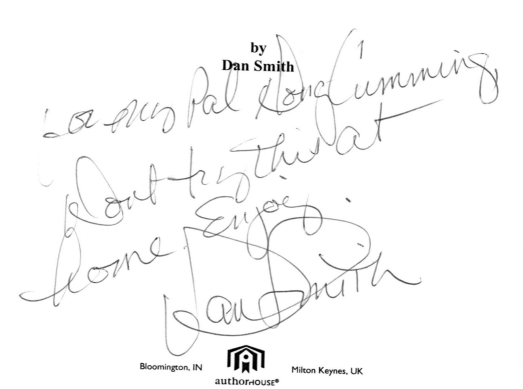

Bloomington, IN   authorHOUSE®   Milton Keynes, UK

AuthorHouse™
1663 Liberty Drive, Suite 200
Bloomington, IN 47403
www.authorhouse.com
Phone: 1-800-839-8640

AuthorHouse™ UK Ltd.
500 Avebury Boulevard
Central Milton Keynes, MK9 2BE
www.authorhouse.co.uk
Phone: 08001974150

First published by AuthorHouse 11/2/2006

ISBN: 1-4259-7118-0 (sc)

Printed in the United States of America
Bloomington, Indiana

This book is printed on acid-free paper.

E-mail the author at editrdan@msn.com

ACKNOWLEDGEMENTS

I suppose it'd be easiest to just go ahead and thank or curse everybody I ever knew—and some I didn't—because each, in some way, helped shaped what's on the following pages. But I'll try to be more immediate and more specific.

My wife, Christina, was the first to wade through a 28-day complete manuscript, to make suggestions, to offer criticisms (Christina's so damn civilized that the criticisms sounded like the entire corps of the University of Tennessee cheerleaders was standing behind her). Christine MacConnell and Melanie Almeder, far better wordSmiths than I (even though I have the name) read various versions and made important suggestions, which made their way into the final product. They helped nip and tuck, combine and form the original mess. The title of the book is Melanie's idea. Originally, it was Some Things I Remember and Some Others That I Don't. See why it's advisable to have sane editors? Good friends Emily Carter and John Montgomery did a thorough job reading proof.

Betsy Gehman, my surrogate mom for about a decade, read the book with the same kind of loving support and sharp-edged observation I value. She was instrumental in bringing out memories I'd forgotten and for helping me find the detail I needed when I needed it. Thanks to Cricket Powell for her truly striking snapshot of an aging, grouchy warhorse that adorns the cover. It's one of my favorite pictures of myself.

To everybody mentioned within the pages of Burning the Furniture and to the ones who didn't make the cut, I have to say, "You're important to me and you're no more important because you're in the book or less important because you're not. It's just a book and it tells some stories I remember. I've held some back for various reasons and some others didn't fit what I was trying to accomplish. But thank you for the joy and the pain and the grief and the good fortune you've all brought me."

This Doug Miller photo was taken in 1986 for The Roanoker
Magazine's story on Baby Boomers turning 40. I looked
pretty good for a guy who drank a double six-pack and
smoked three-and-a-half packs of cigarettes a day

INTRODUCTION

The following pages contain a lifetime of stories from my perspective, one that's often called "creative memoir" when presented this way: a lot of fact mixed with fictionalized accounts. These stories generally happened the way I tell them, at least the way I saw them. Every story has its different perspectives and the only one I've ever felt responsible for is my own.

My mother, always a good storyteller, talked of her tales as being "some truth, some exaggeration and some outright lies getting together to tell how something really was."

Some of these stories have characters with names different from the people these events happened to because I either wanted to protect them or to protect me from them. They know who they are, but you probably won't. At least one story is apocryphal in its detail, though its essence isn't. Creative memoir uses that tactic to get at the reality of a situation, the underlying truth. Fact sometimes takes a back seat to that ultimate truth.

Many of the stories in this book have appeared in other forms and other places, notably on public radio, where I have been writing and reading essays for years, and in the columns I have written for various publications.

Still, mostly what you have is real people being called by their real names in real situations. Some of them you couldn't—or wouldn't want to—make up, anyway.

But, bless their hearts, I love them all because they have given me a life full of wonder, excitement, pain, fury, pleasure, delight and feeling. Those are all good things.

TABLE OF CONTENTS

Part 1: Getting Formed

The Beginning	8
Laughing With Mom	13
Panic Pond	16
Pine Forest Sleds and Kudzu Hideouts	22
The Christmas Bomb	27
'Cut Me a Switch'	31
The Glove	35
Mr. Henry	38
Serious Games	41
The Daisy Red Ryder, Model 1939	47

Part II: Growing Up

Raisin' Hell	52
Daddy Dies	58
The Language of the Sewer	66
The Home	70
Cranberry High	78
Becky and the Baby	84
Coot	94

Part III: Working

The Newsroom	101
The Draft	107
Newspaper Stories	114

Part IV: Love Notes

Rings	132
The Marrying Kind	136
My Favorite Ex-Wife	139

Part V: Have a Drink on Me

Slouching Toward Oblivion   148
Driving Drunk: A Love Story   156
Gettin' Sober   161

Part VI: The End

—30—   174
Oh, One More Thing   176

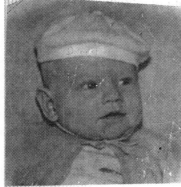

From top left: 4 years old; 5 years old with David, Becky; 8th grade (13); 9th grade (14); with David (9); With David (10); 7th grade (12); 4th grade (9); 5th grade (10)

PART 1:
GETTING FORMED

THE BEGINNING

"If we ever have to move again, I'm going to burn the furniture," my mother said during an especially grueling move from one barely livable rental house to another.

We were always a quick-step ahead of the eviction notice. Moving was the Smith family equivalent of the vacation where our little unit got to visit new places, experience new things, and take part in small adventures on an annual basis.

The moving wasn't so much from town-to-town—though there was some of that—but it was from house-to-house, sometimes just a block over, once or twice next door.

We were always poor, something nobody would have predicted when Mom and Dad were married in 1934, because George Edward Smith was a rarity: a college graduate. He'd earned good grades in Business Administration, was a ranking officer in Virginia Polytechnic Institute's cadet corps, an athlete of note, a handsome, outgoing personality with seemingly boundless energy. His family was well-connected in East Tennessee, where his father, George Washington Smith, was one of the region's most respected general contractors, a man who literally helped build Johnson City. Dad, a strapping 6-footer, married a barely 5-feet-tall, auburn-haired, funny, vivacious beauty from far back in the mountains of Western North Carolina that everybody loved—save Dad's flame-haired, over-protective Irish mother, Mary Catherine Garvin Smith.

But as World War II ended and Dad decided to make the Army his career after serving with a degree of distinction in stateside supply, he ran into a medical problem, which led to deep disappointment, which segued into the breaking of an Army regulation and, ultimately, a year in federal prison.

The dishonorable discharge and prison time sealed any ambition he might have had as a business executive and it sent Dad to the restaurant business where they don't ask questions, but they don't pay, either.

My mother knew poverty first-hand because she grew up without money in an isolated mountain hollow. That probably was the root of Mary Catherine Garvin Smith's frowning disapproval of my mother, Opal Dane McCurry, late of Squirrel Creek in Avery County, N.C., and wife of Mary's blond-haired golden-boy, George. (A brief aside here: McCurry was originally Macquarrie when the family lived on the Isle of Mull in Scotland.)

But the poor people of the mountains were not like the poor people of the city: they had big, extensive families, gardens, cows, tight-knit churches and a world-view that included a lot of people like them. In the city, a poor person only had to walk a few blocks to see a better life: warm homes, shiny cars, good food, bright futures. There was more desperation and destitution in Depression-era city poverty and I don't think Mom ever adjusted. It probably helps explain—beyond the knock of the bill collector—why Mom was constantly on the lookout for another house, another possibility, another chance, one that would change the current circumstance.

*

I was born at St. Joseph's Hospital in Asheville, N.C., in 1946. I suspect Mom went to a Catholic hospital because it was either less expensive than the alternative, or was free to the poor. I was the sixth of eight children and arrived barely 12 years into George's and Opal's marriage. That's a lot of kids in a dozen years (Mom once mentioned two stillborns, but didn't say much about them); especially when you consider that Dad took virtually all of World War II off to be a soldier. By then, Dad and Mom, hauling the children along, had lived in Johnson City (twice), Asheville, Radford, Va., Burlington, N.C., and maybe even a couple of other cities I'm not aware of. Dad had begun his career, following a stint at the munitions plant in Radford, in what was, I think, his first job out of college, working for his friend Paul Wofford (my youngest brother's namesake) at Cherokee

Flooring in Burlington, where his future looked secure before the war started.

But the family moved. And moved. And moved. Especially after Dad's misfortune with the Army and after my birth, which came almost simultaneous to that. We wound up in a hot, humid, provincial, snooty little other-side-of-the-Savannah-River suburb of Augusta, Ga., North Augusta, S.C., when I was five years old, living in a frame house with no yard, behind a little main street restaurant, The Rainbow Grill, where Dad was the manager. The house was old, rambling, treeless, and uncomfortable. Like most people, we didn't have air conditioning, an exotic, expensive luxury, and in summers when the temperature was regularly in the mid-90s with humidity around the same number, fans did nothing but blow hot air. Mom, who was accustomed to the cool summers of Avery County, suffered mightily and complained nonstop. She slowly grew depressed and even as a child I sensed discontent, chronic discontent.

I noticed at a young age that sometimes, when Mom entered a room, the lights seemed to go off.

She had fainting "spells." She wouldn't go out in public because of what was later explained to me as "agoraphobia." Sometimes she was passive-aggressive, but always she was overprotective of us kids, not letting us have bicycles, even when our friends wanted to give us their old one, after Christmas brought a new Columbia. She yelled at us from the back porch to get out of the street ("Play in the yard or come in the house!") and she yelled at us for playing in the house ("It's too pretty for you to be cooped up in here!"). But she was funny, almost always funny, the humor often black and resigned, but still, even for a child, funny. If Mom didn't teach me anything else—and she did—she taught me subtlety in delivering the punch line.

*

One hot summer day when I was five or six, I was playing just outside the imaginary boundaries of the front yard—which had no grass and no fence—at the back of a doctor's office that sat beside the Rainbow Grill. I was climbing on the doctor's large black sedan, a Plymouth I think, and had climbed up the back, reached the level of the window, slipped and fell backwards. I felt a sharp pain, and as I hit the ground, saw blood running over the inside back of my right thigh, just about where my short pants ended. I was terrified and started screaming, climbing to my feet, holding the wide, deep laceration together and scrambling into the house. "I cut my leg off!" I cried just before passing out.

I awoke minutes later in the owner of the Plymouth's office, lying on a table, an old man hovering over my thigh, sewing it together. He had not used anything to deaden the pain and every time he put the needle in, I screamed. This was a deep, six-inch-long cut on the thigh muscle and should have required tiny, tight stitches, maybe 100 of them. But this old quack tossed in half a dozen stitches and dismissed us, knowing we didn't have any money to pay him. My mother was apoplectic, yelling at the old man and he told us to "get out of my office, you white trash!" I didn't know what "white trash" was, but I suspected it didn't equate to "pillar of the community." It was a relatively early introduction to the humiliation that I was discovering accompanies poverty.

The leg has always had a large, stretched scar, but it healed, perhaps in spite of the doctor, rather than because of him. We moved from that house not long after the incident, one that haunted Mom because I was playing 40 feet from the house and doing exactly nothing I wasn't supposed to, except maybe climbing on the car. But she blamed the incident on the house.

The next house was the back half of a frame duplex, sitting in a wooded area with a creek running through it (lousy house, great place to play) and it was followed by another frame house—110 Forest Ave., I recall; telephone number 76533—with a huge back yard that abutted my elementary school's playground. Mom felt good about that. She didn't feel good the day I was trying to make my way home from a pickup baseball game at the school and a mighty wind—the edge of a hurricane—came up. All of us kids stayed too long, trying to finish an inning and by the time we determined we'd better get on home, the wind was up around 60-70 mph and I only weighed about 70 pounds.

As I crossed our back yard, making my way to the rear entrance of the house—a screened porch where I often slept—I heard a loud "CRACK!" and looked up at the house to see Mom standing at the back door screaming and pointing behind me. I leaned into the wind, turned slightly to see a monstrous chinaberry tree slowly falling toward me, fighting the wind as hard as I was. I leaned at about a 45 degree angle and fought with all my strength. I heard the tree crash on the ground behind me, feeling the tips of its upper branches as they brushed my back and knocked me face down. I had missed being mashed into a pink, greasy spot by feet, but worse than that, Mom had witnessed the whole thing and I knew I wouldn't be able to get 10 feet from the house for the next week. I knew, having seen the back-yard threat, she'd start looking for a more suitable, safer house and I didn't want to move again. I liked this place.

So, we moved about two blocks north, then, a few months later, we moved two blocks east and four blocks north, up the hill on Georgia Avenue, the steep hill overlooking downtown North Augusta. Heavily laden cotton trucks would occasionally crest this hill going too fast, lose their brakes about halfway down and wind up screaming into the Savannah River Bridge, ripping out the concrete railing and piling into the river. As a kid, every time I walked across that bridge on the way to a movie in Augusta, I'd break into a dead run and not stop until safely across, thinking a truck was on my butt every step of the way.

The peak performance of Mom's moving career came when she landed us in The Big House, this marvelous Spanish villa at the top of Georgia Avenue, but it was there that Dad died and we wound up—literally and figuratively, going from the top of the hill to the bottom of Georgia Avenue in an aging, fragile Victorian home on the banks above the river, where the town's only real poor people lived. I was 13 years old and we had officially arrived, fatherless, in poverty and with nowhere else to go.

There was some of that nerve-wracking anxiety in each of our moves: When would we have to move again? Where would we go? Who would be after us? Would the next house be a dump?

Certainty and security, for the poor, are as elusive as regard.

Grandpa Smith   **Grandma Mary Smith**

LAUGHING WITH MOM

The last time I saw my mother, she was resting in a wheelchair, breathing with a great deal of difficulty, mostly wheezing, attached to a respirator, tears streaming down her face from the joke she'd just cracked.

The last few years of Mom's life, she was umbilically connected to a tank of oxygen, dragging it after her as she slowly glided from room to room muttering in past tense, reliving lost moments, whistling long-gone tunes in that oddly cheerful way she had, looking for a cigarette.

Mom was never more than a tick from heartbreak, despair, serious clinical depression. It was so devastating that she'd submitted to Electro Convulsive Therapy—"shock treatment"—in the 1950s (her shrink was a guy named Thigpen, who wrote *The Three Faces of Eve*), searching for a good day. Nor was she ever more than the slightest one-line setup removed from a joke, a quick comeback, an outrageous pun.

If ever God put a walking contradiction on earth, it was Mom. Her life had been hard: childhood filled with rural poverty and a tyrannical mother; bearer of eight unplanned, and I suspect that given her choice at the time, unwanted children. She was the wife of an alcoholic who died in middle age, leaving her with nothing except hungry kids to raise, loneliness and desperation. Her depression was so obvious and so overwhelming at times that there seemed to be a gray fog around her. I'd hide when I knew she was having one of her spells. The other kids would disappear, too.

She had agoraphobia before anybody knew what it was, fainting in public rather than facing the terror other people represented. Fainting became a common escape mechanism for her. It became so frequent at one point, that we'd just leave her where she fell until she woke up, providing she hadn't hit anything on the way down. Why disturb her?

But always, there was a laugh at the edge of the disaster or a song in the midst of it. From the time I could walk and remember anything at all, I heard mom sing, hum, whistle, dance and do her version of karaoke to the radio, which was always on—when we had electricity. I have a deep appreciation for 1950s jazz because of that early exposure, a gift she could not have imagined giving me.

Mom had been a small and dazzlingly pretty young woman—one who simply slew my well-to-do dad, a college grad from Johnson City residential construction money who was smitten by her. She'd once had a date with my dad and another guy at the same time and the boys showed up in front of her house bumper-to-bumper, Dad driving his 1932 Ford roadster with the rumble seat, the other guy in an expensive Cord. "I was going with the one who got there first," she later mused, grinning wide, "but they got there together and I was afraid to go outside, so I didn't go with either of them. I told my sister Mabel to tell them I was sick and she said, 'Little girl you got yourself into this; now get yourself out.'" Dad forgave her. The other guy didn't. She got a good story out of it, one she told often.

She'd actually gotten into the car with another suitor at one point, heading toward the church to get married. My would-be gold-digging mom got cold feet. "He had an airplane," she said one day when she was in a storytelling mood. "Rich guy. But dull! Boring. I couldn't stand him. I never saw him laugh once. On the way to get married, I looked over at him, studied him for a minute and said, 'Take me home!' And I didn't say it quiet."

Because Dad couldn't find good-paying jobs, we never had any money and we were always a paycheck away from the street. Our homes were rentals, usually too small, never affording Mom any privacy (me, neither, for that matter; I slept on the screened porch of one house winter and summer, so I wouldn't have to share a bed with my bed-wetting brother). Mom'd dress for bed in her closet. I never knew what Dad thought about that.

All of this led to monumental stress in Mom. Dad didn't seem especially troubled by our poverty, tight living conditions, old drafty houses or much of anything else, even during his seven-year sober period. Dad worked seven days a week, 364 days a year and he usually slept or read on Christmas after the morning festivities. When he got home from work in the afternoons, he'd read a western novel, sometimes two: one before dinner and one after. I always thought that was something admirable.

It seemed odd to me that Mom had more difficulty adjusting to our poverty than Dad had, given their backgrounds. It was wearisome for her even when she was cracking the dark jokes and I suppose the cumulative effect was just too much sometimes.

"We get to camp tonight," she'd say as we arrived from school to a dark house with no heat because there was no money to pay the bills. Or if we came home from school hungry—as we always did—complaining that there was nothing to eat, she'd quickly retort, "We got bread, we got lard, make a sandwich." Then she'd go to the cupboard and create a snack from nothing. Nothing at all. When I was small I thought she was magic.

Magic. Now there's a concept. Maybe Mom knew the magic was in the jokes, in the music. Maybe that's why she died, wheezing out one final joke through the respirator. "If you ever get married again," she rasped, "find a dumb one. You don't seem to have much luck with the smart ones."

Mom and Dad in about 1956. She's ready to crack a joke. I can see it

Panic Pond

Town Council named it the Panic Pond because right smack in the middle of building North Augusta's municipal swimming pool in 1929, the stock market crashed and a kind of national madness took over for a while. People jumped out of Wall Street windows, ran on banks, wondered if God had forsaken them and they were generally in a state.

Meanwhile, the concrete guys were finishing up the lower side of the swimming pool, up near where the ice-cold creek fed in from out of the woods as October bled into November. Town Council thought that, given the circumstances, this big man-made swimming hole with the two bathhouses, sand beach, floating raft, two diving boards, high slide and the state-of-the-art filtering system should give some sort of nod to the national mood. Panic Pond.

I never thought much about the name when I was 10 or so, but it had a familiar ring. I spent every day of every summer for several years in the Panic Pond's cold and suspect waters. I saw my first live breast there, nestled in the blonde girl's teal bathing suit cup that was a size too large for it. I saw my first dead body, a little kid who drowned, pulled from the waters of Panic Pond as a stricken group of people gathered helplessly around, some of them crying out loud, others shouting. I ate frozen Zero bars and taught myself to swim on top of the water after teaching myself to dive and swim *under* water. I learned how it's possible to make just enough money to do a thing you want to do in a short time and I learned that sometimes you have to suffer to get it done.

I grew up a good bit at the Panic Pond, some of the growing naturally, some of it forced, all of it part of the whole deal.

We were living over near North Augusta Elementary School, just behind the playground, that first summer I discovered the Pond. Mike Graybill had asked me over to his house to spend the night and I knew that was something I wanted to do because Mike's parents let him drink coffee and for breakfast he made this great toast with real butter. At home, we only had biscuits and gravy and eggs and grits and bacon and like that. Mom didn't let us drink coffee because she said it was bad for kids, made us nervous. But I'd had coffee before, sneaked it from the Nescafe jar, and it didn't make me nervous. When you put enough cream and sugar in it, I'd found, it tasted pretty good and I liked the way it perked me up, as Mom described its effect.

Mike had told me to bring a bathing suit and I wasn't sure I had one, but Mom bailed me out with an old one of my brother Sandy's. It wasn't much more than a pair of boxer shorts, maybe a little thicker with a net inside to hold my little weenie in place, as if that would be an issue, given that the aforementioned weenie was tiny to begin with and when cold water hit it, it shrank even more. This suit was red with white stripes and it was a little loose on me, but it would do. Later, when it fell to my knees every time I moved suddenly in the water, I wished it was tighter.

Mike didn't tell me where we were going swimming and I didn't ask. His family had a good bit more money than my family and they did things that we didn't do, like going to the beach and going to the swimming pool. I guessed we'd find a pool somewhere, but it never occurred to me that Mike and I would walk two blocks to this giant pool owned by the city—of which Mr. Graybill was the North Augusta waterworks superintendent, a job I thought was big stuff. He was a dour little man with gray hair who was rarely around. His wife was pretty, tall—taller by a good bit than Mr. Graybill—and a good bit younger and she always seemed to have some place to be, too.

By about 8 o'clock Saturday morning of the first night I slept over, Mike and I were in the kitchen by ourselves making coffee and toast with butter and looking ahead to going swimming by ourselves. Mike asked me if I'd brought any money and I said no and he said we'd have to come up with at least a dime to get in and another dime if I wanted to get a Zero bar and a grape Nehi. Lunch would be a quarter for a burger or a hotdog with fries and a drink, but that much money might as well have been a house payment for all the chance I had of coming up with it.

Mike knew that the A&P, two blocks from his house—the other way, away from the Pond—would give us two cents apiece deposit for pop bottles and all we had to do was come up with five bottles for me to get into the Pond and five to get the Zero and Nehi. His dad had given him enough money (I found out later that it was $1, but Mike never was a generous soul), so we only had to think about me.

Bottles were everywhere if you knew where to look. We found them on the side of the road, in people's trash cans, behind the supermarket in its dumpster. I never figured out why the A&P had bottles in its dumpster on one end when it was paying two cents apiece for them on the other end. In any case, I was introduced to recycling as commerce and it became my routine in the morning to get up, scour the countryside for bottles, take them to the cash register at the A&P and head off for the Panic Pond.

Our first trip together to the Pond was on a June morning, probably the second week, because school was out and by this time, the central part of South Carolina is already in full summer heat mode. That meant the asphalt between Mike's house and the Pond presented itself as a major obstacle.

If I didn't know what a "hotfoot" was before we set out that morning, I did by the 10th stride. We were both barefoot because boys didn't wear shoes during the summer in North Augusta, S.C., in the summer of 1956. It simply was not done. I'd sooner have let my hair grow out. So we were taking a few steps on the street, jumping off and into sandy grass, which was full of sandspurs—nasty, spiky creations God must have put in the ground for some kind of vengeance against some terrible wrong. Our choices were not good ones and, later, when we spent the night at my house and had to walk an extra half a mile, it was especially gruesome.

I especially recall that the top of my head—with my short crew cut—and the bottom of my feet—given the asphalt walks—stayed sunburned or streetburned all the summer long and that the Panic Pond's cold waters always felt good, even when I shivered and shriveled.

The Pond itself was a minor wonder of the world to my young mind. It was about 30 yards wide and 100 yards long with a peeling painted aqua concrete wall surrounding three sides. The side near the woods was the most natural, falling off from the edge of the miniature forest, a creek running straight into the Pond and sycamore trees lining the banks on each side of the emptying creek. As we moved to the left from the bathhouses and walked toward the creek, the water turned darker and darker green and vegetation, including some lily pads, became more evident. The usable portion of the pond—the best part for swimming—was probably 30 yards wide, making the swimming pool a square and the swimming hole next to it—complete with mud bottom—a long rectangle.

I always suspected that the water was dangerously nasty, but apparently it was suitable for swimming because occasionally, when the pool opened in the morning, I'd see people taking out water samples in glass containers. They were, I imagined, tested and pronounced swimmable, if not drinkable.

Mike and I'd been swimming every day for weeks by late June, creating our own routine of getting the money first thing in the morning, hot-footing it down, swimming for two hours, breaking for a Zero bar and Nehi, then lying on the beach for 30 minutes or so. The lifeguard told us if we went into the water too quick, we'd get cramps and we'd die before he could get to us. So we sat down for a while. Then we went back into the pond to swim, play tag, dive some, play war, splash the girls, play submarines. I learned to swim and dive by playing, but I didn't learn the skills in the order most people learn them. I dived first because it took the least skill. Out of the dive, it was necessary to swim under water. Swimming on top took a lot of effort and was accomplished last.

Each day at about 1 o'clock, I'd pack up and head home for a quick lunch that Mom would have waiting, and sprint back—on an even hotter road—to the pond.

One day I got back about 2 o'clock and everybody was bunched up in a circle on the beach and people were crying and screaming at each other. "Give him some room!" somebody yelled. "He can't breathe! Back up!" An ambulance roared into the parking lot, its light flashing urgently and two men in white clothes came running to the beach, carrying bags. The crowd opened and the men ran to the center. That's when I saw Timmy Edwards lying there lifeless, his tiny body not moving.

Timmy was the newly adopted five-year-old son of my mother's best friend and he'd been swimming alongside us all summer. He swam like he was born in the water and was a fearless little guy. He laughed and played and was just about as happy and curious a kid as I ever knew. He was lying there light blue, limp and dead. Allen Simmons, a pitcher on my Dixie League baseball team, had stepped on Timmy as Allen climbed up the ladder to the raft at the center of the Pond. Allen had gone under water to see what he'd stepped on and found Timmy, his bathing suit hooked on a nail, drowned. Allen, a big kid, had pulled Timmy loose and swam with him in his arms to the shallow water and then walked him to the beach and lay him down.

Mike and I left Panic Pond that day with our heads down. The sun had gone behind a big cloud and the pavement had cooled as much as it could, so the somber walk home wasn't interrupted by the usual yelps. As we passed Mike's house and he peeled off, I said, "See you tomorrow," and he said, "Yeah, OK," without much feeling.

They closed the pool for two days and we didn't have anything to do for those days, but we didn't mind so much because it was sort of a way of honoring Timmy for being a good little guy. Mom did a lot of cooking for Timmy's parents and she was gone more than usual for a while, over at the Edwards' house, talking to them, I guessed. It was a sad time at home and I heard Mom and Dad whispering late at night and for several evenings, I'd hear what I thought must be Mom crying. Mom almost never cried.

*

When the Pond reopened, I experienced the flip side of the Timmy misery. Mike and I had worked into our routine of occasional walking trips around the pond when the teenaged girls sat on the concrete sides, getting their feet wet, but not going in. We learned that if we walked slowly and looked at just the right times, every once in a while, we could see the top of a breast. Well, on this particular day, a girl named Joanie who was maybe 15 or 16, but built a little larger than most of her contemporaries, was sitting over near the diving board dangling her feet. Every once in a while, almost like clockwork, she adjusted her bathing suit top, which seemed awfully slippy.

So I thought this might be the opportunity of the summer, and danged if it wasn't. Just about the time I passed for the first time behind Joanie, she bent forward and her suit went a little ahead, exposing a *nipple*. It was a whole nipple, pointy, light brown and just the most fantasmagoric thing I'd ever seen. I stood there frozen in mid-step, unable to go any further, staring, feeling a distinct and curious stirring beneath my red stripped bathing suit. But Joanie had her back to me, so she didn't see. Mike saw, though. From across the pond, I caught a glimpse of something moving quickly and here came Mike, knowing exactly what I was looking at and wanting to get in on it. Joanie noticed, too, and she hitched up her top, turned and stared straight into my face. I was mortified, trying to innocently smile, cutting my eyes, continuing my stride, a bit more briskly. Mike ran right up my back, looking—staring—at the top of Joanie's bathing suit. We both hit the deck and the laughter was riotous from the teenagers lined up at the diving board, who saw what we were doing.

Embarrassed, humiliated and scratched up from our fall, we both got up and hurried back to the bathhouse where we escaped into the dressing room and I immediately almost yelled to Mike, "I saw a NIPPLE! God. All. Mighty! A *nipple!* Maaaaaaaaaan!" The conversation didn't reach a higher level, but Mike knew exactly what I was saying. That image would be good for the rest of the summer, for wet dreams and morning boners. I'd see that white breast and that delicate brown pointed nipple on every girl over the age of 10 for months. It was frozen—more solidly than a Zero bar—in my mind. That glimpse of Joanie's breast served as a pre-pubescent sexual delivery system for the foreseeable future.

The end of the season was coming and I couldn't wait for the guys at school to ask about my summer.

Pine Forest Sleds and Kudzu Hideouts

In the southernmost regions of the United States, snow is a theoretical concept, but the lack of snow has never discouraged the Children of the South from sledding in winter, at least if my experience is any indication. The young tend toward resourcefulness and those of the west central South Carolina piedmont regions, where I grew up, are expert sledders, though their sleds and their snow don't resemble what you'd find in Williamsport, Pa., Binghamton, N.Y., or Ames, Iowa.

In my South, people tended to do things their own way, sometimes flying in the face of convention, sometimes just making do with something different. Look at automobile racing, for example. Southerners took what was essentially an upper-crust, elitist, rich playboy's sport and turned it over to chicken farmers and moonshiners. They created NASCAR and of course NASCAR fans are courted by presidential candidates from New England these days.

That's not to say that sledding on South Carolina snow is worth much more than a warming thought on a cool night, but it certainly is worth all of that.

So how's a kid going snow sledding with neither snow nor sled? Simple: South Carolina snow falls in the form of long, slick Southern Pine needles. These nearly foot-long brown needles pile an inch deep in large pine forests that dot the rolling hills on the western boundary of the state. The acidity of the needles discourages forest floor growth of small plants that would get in the way of sleds, and there are wide swaths of forest without obstacles and those are often pointed downhill.

So, nature provided two of three elements necessary for good sledding: a slick surface and a slope.

People's Drug Stores provided—when I was a boy—the third element: cardboard boxes, which became our sleds. The medium-sized boxes, flattened out with all seams unglued, were best for 10-year-olds. They were sleek and fast and easy to maneuver if you knew how to bend the front corners to your cupped hand and use them as a steering wheel.

The front flap, which already had a crease, was pulled to the knees of the sitting child and curled slightly over them. Then the corners were bent forward so they could be held as the driver leaned right or left in steering.

The sleds were as fast as any snow sled I've ever seen and could whip around a tree without slowing down.

At the bottom of my favorite hill was a small ravine with a slight rise on either side of the four-feet-wide, two-feet-deep ditch. If I got enough speed coming down the hill, I could sail over the ravine in the same way a skateboarder leaps around urban landscapes today. One day I hit that baby just right after an uninterrupted run straight down the hill and landed in a small bush about 20 feet beyond the ditch, flying through the air just long enough to yell, "Geronimoooooooooooooo!" I busted my skinny butt, but I was a hero for a day to the other kids. That was quite a leap.

Another day I banged off a bulky pine halfway down the run and that knocked my path off kilter, spinning around and becoming disoriented for an instant. I steered back toward the path, never losing any speed, and overshot it, hitting another tree, skinning my knuckles, which were holding up the curled front edge of the cardboard sled. I was starting to get scared because I was out of control and going faster with each smashup. As I hurtled toward the bottom of the hill, screaming more intensely with every foot and—I thought—facing death, I saw that I was to the left of the ditch jump and heading fast at a brush pile that would flip me into the gulley. I tugged, pulled and pleaded with the sled until it turned slightly right, edged into the beaten path and, at the last possible instant, hit dead center on the jump, cleared the gulley by what felt like half a mile and landed as if I had a parachute on. The boys at the top of the hill cheered. I fell spread-eagle backwards and laughed out loud.

The guys in my pack invented sledding races of all kinds, ball games for a downhill run; and there was war—any war'd do, didn't matter—and games of cowboys 'n' Indians. I liked being an Indian because the clothes and weapons were more appealing— and I could make both from odds and ends lying around.

There was the occasional voyage of the luxury liner when one in the gang came up with a major appliance box. Refrigerator boxes were treasured because not only would they hold 10 kids, but they had lid-like tops and bottoms that, when removed, served as life boats or individual sleds for the small children. They didn't steer well, but they were sturdy, slow and safe.

On those days when we had two or more of the big boxes—with windows and gun portals cut into the sides—great sea battles or tank wars were staged. But that didn't happen often because there was a lively competition for the boxes from a number of the kids in our small town.

Cardboard box sledding had it all over what the Yankee kids did, at least on a couple of levels. It was never wet and it was never cold. But I never made ice cream out of pine needles, either.

*

When the sledding season waned and heat became an issue, it was to the top of the trees for us. These trees—most of them about the size of a dogwood because a lot of them were dogwoods—were covered in kudzu, the Japanese vine brought to the Philadelphia Expo in the 1890s that Southern adults hate and kids love. The adults know that kudzu grows two feet a day in the deep South and can cover a farm house over the course of a long vacation break. They know you can't kill it any more than you can kill honeysuckle and that kudzu kills trees and dominates everything it touches, including electrical wires. The power company can be added to the list of those who hate it.

Kids love kudzu—did when I was a kid, anyway—because of what it led us to create: forts in the sky where legendary wars were fought on hot, buggy summer days and evenings. When kudzu took over a grove of trees, "woods" to a kid, it grew to the tops and spread out. That created a carpet on the crest of the trees and those of us weighing about 70- 85 pounds walked on it, climbed through it, hid above and below it, shot our BB guns at each other—to our mothers' stark horror—while hiding in it.

I'd occasionally go to the top of the trees by myself just to lie in the kudzu, springy as a bed, and watch cloud formations, a dinosaur here, a fireman there, a dog and a horse and a castle. When we played games and I was on top, an occasional head would pop through or some kid walking on top would disappear with a yelp.

Mike Graybill, Marion McCorckle, Peter Hunt, me and a couple of other boys were playing our version of what Marion called "Cowboys and Niggers" (he could be a nasty little jerk) and the rest of us referred to simply as "war" one bright June day in about 1958—I'd have been about 12. Marion was lying in wait on the roof of one of the kudzu neighborhoods, poking his head down through the top layer and scouting the floor of the woods every little bit, hanging onto his Daisy Air Rifle with a death grip, his hand on the trigger and the gun cocked and ready to put another kid's eye out.

I was one of Marion's enemies that day—and most other days—and I'd caught on to his trap when I saw a sag in the canopy and a dark shadow in the shape of a boy, backlit through the layers of kudzu. Marion wasn't quite as sharp or as treacherous as he imagined.

Mike climbed a tree about 10 feet in front of Marion and I clamored up one about 10 feet behind him. I had a long rope with me—one we used to play cowboys with in a twist of irony—and when we reached the kudzu roof, I looked over at Mike, signaled that the end of the rope was coming and threw it through several branches. It was a great throw, worthy of our own private baseball league, which met most afternoons behind the elementary school, and he caught it as it shot through the branches holding Marion in place.

I grinned. He grinned. I held up a hand and counted off: one, two, three and we jumped, holding the end of the rope and falling through the trees. Each of us stopped as if we were hitched to a bungee cord about three feet off the ground, balancing each other at each end and pulling the roof from underneath Marion, who felt his foundation open up and watched as the floor of the woods rushed to meet his face. Several branches broke his fall, but not his scream. You could hear him over at the grocery store a good quarter of a mile away. I know that because Mom asked me that evening what was wrong with Marion—she'd picked out his high-pitched yelping; I don't know how she did what she did, but boy! did she ever know what was going on—and I said, "Oh, nothing. He fell off one of those little kudzu bushes."

I don't remember anybody ever getting hurt, including Marion that day (I'm not counting ego bruises) but I'm sure some of us did—maybe even me. The pleasure blocks the possibility of pain in this case. A bed in the clouds. Marion McCorckle taking a tumble. Hiding dangerous activities from Mom. Jeeze, no wonder we didn't want to grow up.

THE CHRISTMAS BOMB

It was nearing noon, seven days before Christmas, 1954, and school would let out for the holiday in minutes. My brothers and I had a plan. It was on the edge of being implemented.

Christmas inevitably meant resourcefulness for all of us in the Smith family. Dad had to carefully manage income and Mom had to shop for bargains, beginning at 50 percent off, if there was going to be any Christmas at all.

And the tree—that was mine and my brothers' responsibility. Ever since I was in first grade, two years before, my brothers and I had waited in the woods behind the school for the teachers to toss out each classroom's tree as we broke for the holiday. Some of the trees, most often small pines, came fully decorated. Those were aggressively sought by our competitors, one group of whom didn't want a tree so much as it wanted us not to have one.

Ralph, Earl and Tinker were the boys we wanted to avoid. They were sixth-graders and a lot bigger than my brothers Sandy and David and eight-year-old me. Sandy was 10, David 9. Our three adversaries didn't much like us, didn't much like anybody. They knew Christmas tree procurement was our job and it was important to us. The sport for them was to impede us, to prevent us from taking home a big decorated fir.

Their challenge meant that we'd have to plan, scheme, connive to win. We were too little to simply beat them up; we'd have to outsmart them and I knew, even then, that there was a lot more satisfaction in humiliation of a bully by being smarter than he was than in being bigger and nastier.

Sandy, David and I had talked well into the night preceding our adventure. We settled on a plan that was delicious in its simple intricacy, its deviousness and its timing. One small slipup and we'd fail. That would mean no Christmas tree for the first time. David was the lynchpin of the plan and I suppose that in other circumstances there might have been some concern, since he had been identified as "retarded" by the school system. We knew David better than those tight-assed, bun-wearing, old-maid schoolteachers and administrators and we were betting on him.

The lunchroom of our elementary school, built in the late 1920s or early '30s, was on the third floor of the brick monstrosity of a building. At the back of the lunchroom was an old-style fire escape, a big, metal tube that we jumped in and slid down to safety behind the school and at the edge of the woods. The fire escape had become a kind of theme park ride for us on weekends. Because the school was locked, we had to climb up the escape from the bottom, usually in bare feet because shoes and socks were too slippery. When we reached the top, which was just under the terra-cotta roof, we sat on waxed paper and slid lickety-split down. It was a 75-foot rush.

My classroom was on the third floor; Sandy's was on the second floor; and David's was at ground level in his "special class," the one where these educational Neanderthals herded people who were "different." The bathrooms were on the first and third floors. The bathroom on my level was accessible through the lunchroom.

At 11:55, my hand shot up and I said, "Miss Anderson, may I go to the restroom?"

"Can't you wait five minutes?" she said, in something of a huff.

"No, ma'am," I said, squirming with as much urgency as I could generate. "I really gotta go." Both hands were in my lap.

"OK," she said. "That'll be your Christmas present from me."

Thanks a lot, Miss Generous Spirit of Christmas, I thought, as I scrambled out of my seat and hurried down the hall. Sandy met me at the door of the lunchroom and we hurried toward the back left corner. Miz Washington, probably the first Black person I ever knew and our school's chief cook, was just leaving. Actually, we hadn't figured on her being there at all, since lunch wasn't scheduled that day, but she had been at the school for 30 years, and the faculty was going to have a combination Christmas-anniversary party for her after the students left for the day, in just a few minutes.

We stopped short and looked at her. "Merry Christmas, boys," she said cheerfully as she passed us. We looked at each other, mentally wiping the sweat from our brows, and charged through the door toward the boys' bathroom. We stopped briefly on the other side, waited about 10 seconds and re-entered the lunchroom a few steps from the fire escape's small, white wooden swinging doors. Sandy went in first and I followed quickly. Then we waited.

After a long two minutes, the bell rang and we heard the young celebrants screaming and running from the school, full of freedom and anticipation. We knew our teachers wouldn't miss us or even suspect anything amid the confusion of school closing for the holidays. Sandy and I sat patiently for about 15 minutes. It was quiet on the third floor, but we knew we had a good two hours to go before we could slide out and pick up our tree.

Presently, as we fidgeted and shifted, we heard a rustling at the bottom of the fire escape. Teachers were bringing out their trees and tossing them into a pile. We had scouted each classroom and we knew the tree we wanted: it was from Miz Crutchfield's second-grade class, a seven-foot beauty, the only spruce in the school and a blue spruce at that. All the poor kids would covet that one. Ralph, Earl and Tinker would consider themselves appointed by God to keep us away from it.

Sandy and I continued our restless wait, patience growing short. He punched my shoulder and said, "Get over to your side. You don't own this fire escape." I backed up as much as I could and tried to be still.

Another hour went by. Except for occasional brief skirmishes at the bottom of the fire escape when our adversaries leapt from cover to pummel and chase some of the neighborhood kids away from the trees, it was tomb quiet and the dark of the tubular fire escape intensified the eerie feel.

Finally, we heard what we were waiting for. Boom! Boom-boom-boom! It sounded like cannons going off. Then again, another series: Boom! Boom-boom-boom! It was louder this time and we heard Earl yell, "What the hell is that?" His partners, using forbidden language that the bad guys always used in those days, said, "Shit! Let's go see." Reeling from a double-barreled blast of cuss words, we listened to the telling sounds as they scrambled down from their tree perches at the edge of the woods and ran toward the front of the school building.

Sandy didn't hesitate. He pulled his waxed paper from the back pocket of his blue jeans, put it between his butt and the floor of the escape tube and sailed down. I was a few feet behind him. Sandy hit the ground running—a practiced technique we'd both developed through many hours of sliding these tubes—and I was less than a second in the rear.

As we suspected, Miz Crutchfield had thrown her Best in Show tree on the top of the pile. The faculty party had been in her room and she'd left the tree up until the songs and toasts were over. It was fully decorated with popcorn strings, foil tinsel and icicles, crape paper balls hung by paper clips, cotton pulled flat and placed on branches as snow. It was topped by a pretty angel Mary Anne Thompson had made. She'd shown it to me on the way to school one day and I told her how pretty it was. Mary Anne moved away in the spring, but she stayed long enough to give me my first kiss.

Sandy instinctively went to the front of the tree, stuck his hand inside the limbs and grabbed the trunk. I went to the base and picked up the heavy part. We worked in perfect unison, lifting the tree without dropping a single decoration, and running with it as fast as we could toward 110 Forest Avenue. A smiling Mom, waited at the back screen door, the one that squealed so loud, we'd often hear it open before we heard her voice yelling for us.

David, the boy everybody underestimated, sat smugly on the sofa as we entered the living room. He grinned. "Got a couple of them left," he said, pulling the cherry bombs from his pocket. "Good thing we didn't use all of them July 4. You should have seen those three bums trying to figure out what was making all the noise. I put the cherry bombs in that big metal trash can out front and lay it on its side, pointing toward the back of the school. I hung around just to see them, and, boy, did they look confused."

"I'd bet they were confused when they went back the trees," I said. "When we pulled this one off, the pile looked a lot smaller."

We laughed and slid the tree into its stand. Mom went to the basement to get those wondrous, multi-colored, used car lot lights we always strung on the tree. It was Christmas again and our wait for Santa would be much easier with the big blue spruce sparkling in the corner.

'Cut Me a Switch'

Mom was standing on the back porch, hands on her hips, glaring at me. "Daniel Elbert Norman Smith!" she bellowed, employing the dread, seldom-used full Christian name. "Cut me a switch and cut it thick and long! I have told you until I'm blue in the face that you are to be home before dark!"

"But Mama," I whined, "we were playing baseball and the score was tied. I couldn't just leave."

"Don't talk back to me, young man," she said, breaking into the middle of my last two words and cutting me off, a way of emphasizing that boys shouldn't act this way. "Cut it and get in here with it right now. Don't you slip off and put on another pair of pants or fill your pocket with leaves, either."

Mom knew the absurdity of the drill and I could see her eyes laughing as she warned me.

I was the sixth kid, the underdeveloped, underappreciated and underestimated son, the one she had so thoughtlessly dismissed in a conversation with a friend I'd overheard in recent days. "Opal," marveled the friend, "I don't know how you manage to keep up with eight children and still look good." Mom loved flattery and she replied, "Oh, Mabel, anything after five doesn't make much difference anyway." Here I stood, sensitive, freckled, burr-headed, 50 pounds of kid counting up on my fingers my place in the order of things, then staring blankly into space for a full minute before recovering from the reality of the math.

Mom and I danced our "cut me a switch" dance almost daily as I tried to grow up, packaged as I was between five older brothers and sisters and two younger ones. I don't know why it always seemed to come down to me and that switch. Years later Mom admitted that I was, as she phrased it, "a good little boy, never any trouble." But that was usually when she was talking to one of her girlfriends and to admit to having "a bad little boy, lots of trouble" might have implied that something was amiss in her mothering genes.

Anyhow, I got pretty good at cutting a switch without any stings in it and developed quick-change skills that would've impressed a stage actor. I could cut an impressive-looking, but thoroughly impotent, switch and slip on a pair of my bigger brother's blue jeans in the time it took a normal kid to find a tree. Mom never hurt me—and I'm sure she never intended to hurt me, given the delicacy with which she lashed me and the underlying humor of the whole procedure—but the ritual was written in mist and having been writ, was followed flawlessly.

Mom never threatened me with "wait 'til your daddy gets home" because she knew I would've laughed. Casting Dad as a heavy was like demonizing Howdy Doody. My father was just about the mildest-mannered man I ever knew and the only time I ever saw him mad about anything was the time my slightly older brother Sandy said something nasty to Mom about dinner. Dad got up from his chair, walked purposefully across the room, picked up my brother by the top of his shirt and slammed him so hard into the wall that air came out of him and a crack climbed the plaster. Holding Sandy there, pinned against the wall, Dad calmly said, "If I ever hear you talk like that again to your mother…" He didn't finish the sentence. He didn't need to. Sandy's wide eyes told Dad all he needed to know.

Mom was an occasional creative genius at threat, perception and real punishment in her effort to manipulate her tribe (she was a creative genius at dinnertime, too, often facing semi-empty cabinets and still whipping up an inviting meal, but that's another story). Getting us up in the morning is a good example. Parents can spend a considerable portion of their lives attempting to raise sluggish, sullen, apparently near-death teenagers from bed on school days. Mom gave us one yell. Next step was the cold, wet washcloth on the feet. That was generally good for a wakeup and an "Awwwww, Mama!" after which I'd promptly turn over and go back to sleep. Five minutes later Mom was back with a glass of water, which she would pour into my face. It took little time to connect the steps—like

Pavlov's Dog—and work out the timing so that my feet hit the floor as I heard her walking down the hall with the glass of water. It's easy to underestimate the shock to the system of a cold washcloth, let alone water splashing off a sleeping face (sometimes causing me to pee inadvertently, adding humiliation to the discomfort).

Mom was never mean or cruel, harsh or brutal. In fact, there were times when we were both laughing as she applied one of her unusual punishments. Even the switch became a neighborhood joke, and I can see her standing at the back door, creaking screen door in her left hand, right hand on her hip, reciting the list of names of her children until she got to the one she wanted. Then to our utter mortification, came the Christian name. All of it.

I never was much good at punishing my children. I spanked my son and my daughter a total of once each during their childhoods and I vividly remember both. In fact, when I spanked the three-year-old Evan, he looked up at me with those sad brown, tearing eyes and said, "Spank me some more, Dad. I been a bad boy," and I damn near died.

Evan's mother—that would be Chris, wife No. 2 or so—occasionally manipulated the children's behavior, unintentionally I think, simply by walking into the kitchen. The kids ran screaming to me, "Dan! [Jennie has always called me by my first name.] She's in the kitchen! She's not going to cook is she? Pleeeeease, make her get out. We'll be good." Chris didn't cook well. She once served unsoaked, broiled salt mackerel for dinner. Her mother made a four-dish lunch for us based in lime Jell-O (Jennie and I excused ourselves and went to Burger King), so it must have been hereditary: the anti-kitchen gene.

But Chris could punish in the harshest non-violent (in the physical sense) manner I've ever seen. "Evan," she'd say with that Northern European, puritanical glare, "that will go on your Permanent Record." Permanent Record. My goodness, such a thing to say to a kid. I could see Evan's little mind trying to wrap around the concept, flames boiling up around it, a woman with a tight bun administering it, dozens of brown steel file cabinets locked against the inquiry of the casually interested. Official Business Only. Son, You're In Trouble Now!

Jennie'd look straight at her relentless, lecturing stepmother and plead, "Would you please just spank me and get it over with? Use a belt or a baseball bat if you want. I can't take this." And, boy, could I identify. I heard it, too, when I stepped out of line: "Yanh, yanh, yanh, yanh, yanh, and I think you'll agree, yanh, yanh, yanh, yanh, yanh."

Mom would never have resorted to the lecture. She was too gentle and kind a soul for that type of brutality. Four words would do: "Cut me a switch!"

'Danny Smith, cut me a switch!'

THE GLOVE

The Wilson Fieldmaster Jimmy Piersall model baseball glove was between my eyes and the sun as the ball descended, but as I adjusted at the last instant, the sun shot through a small opening in the web straight into my face, and the ball glanced off the center of my head. I was out cold for long seconds and by the time I awoke, Dad was kneeling over me and Mom was rushing out the back door.

I was forever getting plonked in the head with baseballs, but Mom was furious with Dad. "He's way too little for you to be hitting those old baseballs to," she snapped, grossly underestimating what an 11-year-old should be able to do with a fly ball. It was just that I wasn't much good at it. Dad, who'd been a ballplayer in college, never hit another fly to me. He died two years later. But the Jimmy Piersall model Fieldmaster was with me for many summers after that, smelling of Murphy oil, hanging off the belt of my jeans.

It was a personal piece of little boy gear of the 1950s. Nearly everybody had a glove, even those who couldn't afford one. I was a catcher, but still had a fielder's glove, which was not unusual. The team provided the catcher's mitt and you couldn't really play catch with that fat thing anyway.

When I played organized league ball, I was a catcher. I don't know why, except maybe one day we needed a catcher and I couldn't play infield, outfield or pitch too well. But I could hit, so I probably was an asset overall if you could hide me somewhere that I wouldn't miss flies or grounders.

I stayed a catcher until this jerk coach named Jack Rothrock, a former Jarhead Marine whose father played for the old St. Louis Cardinals Gas House Gang (right field; I looked it up because I didn't believe Jarhead) told me one day to swap gear with Mike Graybill, our pitcher who wasn't throwing so good.

"I'm no pitcher, Mr. Rothrock," I said, more bewildered than upset. "Mike's doing fine, he's just not warmed up yet." I wasn't sure what "warmed up" meant, but it sounded reasonable. I'd heard it before somewhere.

"Listen, Smith," said this big, bulky burrhead calling a child by his last name, "let's get one thing straight: I coach, you follow directions. Savvy? Swap gear and do it doubletime and don't question me. You'll thank me someday."

I got the first part and we exchanged baseball gear. I have never understood what he meant that I'd thank him someday, but he was always saying that.

It took about five rudderless pitches from me to convince Jarhead that Mike at his worst was better than me at my anything. "Jeezy H. Whizzers!" yelled the ex-Marine, who bordered on unacceptable language all the time, but never crossed the line. "Smith, dad-blame it, put that catcher's gear back on! Graybill, get back to the mound and throw the ball straight! You two are the sorriest ..." He didn't finish the sentence, but we knew what he was trying to say.

I got back into my chest protector, shin guards, mask and oversized glove, which hid my humiliation.

But none of this was my Jimmy Piersall Wilson Fieldmaster's fault. It lay on the bench through the whole scene, waiting to be used, knowing it wouldn't be unless one of the other guys needed it.

Baseball gloves—where when I grew up, anyway—were community property, especially during a game. If a kid didn't have a glove for a pickup game, the guy on the opposing team at the same position would leave his glove at that spot as the inning changed. A second baseman, for example, would put his glove on the bag and the other team's second baseman would use it.

My brother, David, didn't have a glove and he was one of the luckier guys in that situation because he was ambidextrous, so it didn't matter if the glove left at his spot was a lefty or a righty.

My Piersall model, as it turns out, was something of an odd coincidence, since my mother was nuts and my dad was a boozer. Piersall wrote the book *Fear Strikes Out*, which became a movie, in which he courageously told everybody about his nuttiness. It wasn't something people talked about in the 1950s. My mother liked Piersall, a man she would normally have known nothing about, for that book. Tony Perkins played Piersall in the movie version of the book (before playing Norman Bates in "Psycho") and Mom loved it, too.

Piersall later became the general manager of a Roanoke minor league football team called the Buckskins, whose play resembled some degree of illness, whether or not mental.

The glove, though, was a thing of beauty in the eye of this beholder. I kept that old stinky hunk of drying leather for a long, long time and only discovered that one of my early wives sold it at a yard sale after the fact. She got a dime for it, she boasted. I lost a glove before I should have and she lost a husband before she wanted to.

I hope the Piersall was bought by some poor kid who gave it a name—"Norman" would be nice—and played with it until it was worn through. I suspect, though, that a collector or an antiques dealer bought it and it's on a shelf somewhere.

'I'm no pitcher, Mr. Rothrock'

Mr. Henry

The Carolina Theater was at the bottom of Georgia Avenue, across the street from the Rainbow Grill, and it was there that I got my first lesson in race relations. We had few people of African extraction in North Augusta, so even seeing somebody who wasn't white was an event, except for Mr. Henry, who was at the movies, in the balcony, just about every time I went.

In those few years of my early childhood before television became part of my family's furniture (that would be 1954), my pals and I went to Carolina every Saturday where triple features were shown until nearly dark. The Carolina was a 1930s-era on-street brick movie house that had a glass-enclosed smoking room and another glassed room for babies, both on the main floor. The theater also had several "love seats," double seats in the back where teenagers sat and smooched.

The non-descript B westerns, thrillers, monster movies and adventure stories my buddies and I enthusiastically attended were all pretty much the same: thin on plot, heavy on action, much like the blockbusters of today.

Because there was such a sameness to the plots, we didn't feel any special responsibility to watch the movie, unless the monster was making an appearance for the first time. We found other ways to amuse ourselves: running the aisles and climbing over the seats, back to front and front to back; going into the glass-enclosed smoking rooms at the back of the auditorium; yelling and screaming and munching popcorn and Raisinettes; and going to the bathroom again and again.

One day, we sneaked up to the balcony where the colored people sat. That became our regular Saturday adventure. It was prohibited, but we didn't know why and we thought it terribly unfair.

A small, but prominent sign at the front of the theater just under the ticket office said, "Whites" and had an arrow pointing to the left. Beside it, a sign read, "Colored" and showed an arrow pointing to the right. Colored people, which is what the more polite among us called our African-American brethren, climbed a staircase accessible from the side of the theater.

There was another stairway behind the concession stand, the one the projectionist used, but we never saw it, only heard dark rumors of its existence. It was accessible through what I was told—in a whisper by the ticket girl—was a *secret door*.

From the moment my buddies and I were aware there was a balcony, we wanted to be in it, and we immediately set to figuring how we'd do it. It wasn't that hard, actually. Because we were all small—maybe four-and-a-half-feet tall—we could duck-walk in front of the ticket booth and never be seen by the blonde girl inside. There were so few colored people attending matinees that there was no usher at the door. The ticket seller ripped their tickets in half and they went upstairs unattended. That meant nobody was guarding the door against short, white, crew-cut, freckle-faced interlopers.

It was a free pass.

Sometimes, we were in the balcony alone. Much later I wondered why a colored person would be interested in a Gene Autry movie, in the first place. If there were any Black people in the movie, they would have been portrayed as ignorant oafs or as mammies.

Often, though, there was this tall, thin, bald old man, who always had on a light-colored suit with a dark—elegant, I thought—hat, which he rested in his lap, and who chewed on a cigar he never lit. Mr. Henry, as we learned to call him, never knowing if that was his first or last name, was always alone and he sat in the same seat: first row, left, on the aisle. It was a great seat and we usually parked as close to him as we could get. The front row was nearest to the giant movie screen, up against the balcony rail, which Mike and I liked to lean over, pretending to spit on bald heads and occasionally spilling a few kernels of popcorn. When the popcorn went over, we'd jerk back muffling a giggle, hide for a brief instant, then slip our heads up to the edge to see who'd been hit and whether he was mad.

One Saturday morning, Mike Graybill dropped his whole box of popcorn on a little man with a shiny head, big glasses and a temper. The man, who had herded several children into the theater, but sat alone as the kids roamed the aisles, complained to the usher, who stormed up the back stairway to investigate. We could hear the rustling downstairs, then the loud thump of shoes coming up the wooden steps. It scared us.

Mr. Henry looked at Mike and me for a moment, then pointed a long, crooked finger toward the back of the balcony and the smoking room. Nobody was inside and Mr. Henry, Mike and I were the only people outside. We scrambled up the aisle and slipped into the booth on the left, going directly to the front floor and sitting there as still as we could be. Both Mike's parents and mine smoked, so we didn't choke on the residual fumes.

We heard the usher talking to Mr. Henry in harsh, but muffled tones that we could make out through the tinny speakers in the closed, smelly room and, shaking in fright, we peeked over the ledge and looked through the cigarette smoke-stained glass. The usher was a big teenager with a round, red face and a pitted complexion, whom we knew to be a football player over at the high school.

"Listen, old man," the usher said, "the owners said we had to let you niggers in here but I ain't never liked it and I ain't gonna like it as long as you act like trash. Throwing stuff out of the balcony onto white people just ain't gonna make you welcome at the Carolina Theater as long as I'm here. So we're gonna throw your back ass out and you ain't never coming back, you understand?" Mr. Henry nodded and reached for his hat.

The usher held Mr. Henry by the upper arm, far too tightly, pulling him toward the stairway, saying something else harsh to him that we couldn't understand through the glass.

We never saw Mr. Henry again.

SERIOUS GAMES

I went most of my life wearing a certain level of distaste for baseball, partly because of that incident with Jack Rothrock where he made me pitch, then humiliated me when I didn't do it well. That and the fact that baseball's slow, stolid, inflexible, hide-bound and I wasn't much good at it.

But, boy, my dad loved baseball. He'd been a pretty good player as a kid, then later in college. At the restaurant where he worked, he and the customers—a lot of them doctors, since the tiny 15-stool, four-booth diner was inside a drugstore at a medical center in Augusta, Ga.—talked baseball while they ate and he cooked.

Dad was a knowledgeable sports guy in general. The doctors relied on his understanding of college football to determine where they'd place their bets with local bookies. Dad knew a lot more than sports and always insisted that "educated man" meant that a guy could talk with some degree of knowledge to just about anybody about danged near anything. He could, I'd say, because he read so much and because he was interested in it all.

It was baseball that got Dad out of the house on those rare occasions that he went anywhere in the evenings, other than West Texas in a Zane Grey novel. During one eight-year stretch while I was growing up—which was most of the time I knew him, since he died when I was 13—Dad went to AA meetings about once a week. He'd pull out that old dark—I couldn't tell exactly what color it was—three-piece suit and carefully put it on. I watched him tug at the jacket, which didn't quite meet where his former washboard stomach had discovered middle age and too many biscuits and gravy.

On baseball nights, when Dad was going with his buddy, the grocery store meat-market manager, to see the Augusta Pirates of the South Atlantic League, or "Sally" League (a team Ty Cobb had played for 50 years earlier), he'd be giddy, cracking wise and belting that big laugh out of his belly as Mom skittered around trying to get him out of the house.

Mom busied herself with boiled or roasted peanuts that she put into a mid-sized grocery bag, Dad being a man of large appetite. Ball clubs let you bring your own food in, which was a good thing because, with our limited income, Dad would likely have gone without. He never made much more a year than $5,500 a year—little even by the standards of the time—and he sure worked for it.

Dad begged and pleaded for years for Mom to go to a ballgame with him, but she wasn't interested, to begin with, and had all those danged children to take care of, besides. Then one night, I watched her get ready while the peanuts were roasting and asked, "Where you going, Mama?"

"I'm going to the baseball game with your daddy and I want you kids to behave yourself and for you to watch Becky and Paul and don't let them get hurt."

"Me, why me?" I whined. "Why don't you make Sandy do it?"

"Danny"—Mom was the last person on earth allowed to call me that god-awful name—"just do what I ask you to do this once without arguing about it. You know I never go anywhere and I want you to help me this once."

That shamed me out of a comeback.

Next morning, about 7 o'clock, I responded to frying bacon and baking biscuits—God-almighty, her biscuits were good—by rolling out of bed and making my way to the kitchen before the other kids woke up. Mom was standing at the stove, pancake turner in hand signing a Vaughn Monroe tune, "Racing With the Moon"—she sang almost all of her waking hours—looked over at her half-awake son and smiled. "What brings you out of that warm bed before I have to threaten you?" she asked, a wide smile greeting me.

"How was the ballgame?" I said, more eager to know than I had imagined.

"Well," she drawled. "We got there, sat down, ate some peanuts, talked a while, ate some more peanuts and talked some more. Your daddy went to the bathroom and when he came back, we ate some more peanuts and talked. Finally, after what seemed like hours, I said, 'George, when is this game going to start?'

"He looked straight at me, sort of puzzled, and said, 'Honey, it's in the seventh inning.' I never saw anything so slow in my life."

' Course, she didn't go back, but that didn't interfere with her serving as support for those of us who did.

*

One late afternoon, I barreled into the house to get ready for a Dixie League baseball game—we didn't have Little League because the national Little League guys had decided to let colored children play with white children, after barring a Black South Carolina team from the World Series and getting a lot of heat for it, so our geniuses had determined that a league of our own would be a good thing. Mom was at her usual perch at the stove, flipping hamburgers and watching French fries brown. Boy, did it smell good!

"Mama, I got a game in a few minutes and I have to get ready," I said, a little too hurriedly.

"Slow down," she said. "You're gonna give yourself a stomach ache." That would have been Mom's way of telling me not to stress myself out and get acid indigestion before I even ate. "The ball field's at the end of the back yard," she said, noting a truth, since our yard butted up against the eastern edge of the schoolyard where we played. "You'll get there."

I slipped on the uniform—actually a dark blue T-shirt with "Posey's Funeral Home" across the front in white felt and a blue hat with a "P" in the middle—Dixie League wasn't big-time yet—and rushed back to the kitchen. "Danny, don't hover. You'll get burned," Mom said.

"Uh," I said, hesitating. "Can I take some supper to the game?"

"If you can carry it, sure," she said, relenting a lot quicker than I expected.

I grabbed three hamburgers—I was little, but hungry—and started stuffing French fries into my pants pocket. "Danny Smith! What in God's good world are you doing?" Mom hollered.

I turned and sprinted out the door, as she yelled after me. A few minutes later I sat on the bench, munching on my burgers and pulling mashed fries out of my grease-stained pockets. Jarhead Rothrock looked at me like I had two heads and said, "Smith"—I always had trouble with people calling nine-year-olds by their last name—"get your gear on." I popped another fry, smiled and started buckling on the shin guards.

I hit three home runs in that game—Dixie League home runs meant that the outfielder missed the ball and the runner kept running; nobody kept a count on errors because nobody could count that high—and when I showed up back at the house, broadly smiling afterwards, Mom met me at the screen door on the back porch with, "Well, how was supper, Mickey Mantle?" Mom always knew what to say to keep that ego from becoming inflated. She gave tribute just the same and, apparently, she'd slipped down to the end of the back yard and sneaked a peek without me knowing. I liked that.

*

Baseball games weren't always league-regulated for my pals and me. More often, we'd play pickup, since Dixie League was only two days a week, and because we were poor, we didn't always have bats and balls, so we had to improvise.

One hot Saturday afternoon, a bunch of us exited the woods at the end of the schoolyard after finishing a game of war and somebody said, "Let's play some ball."

It never occurred to anybody that we had no equipment with us. One of the guys picked up a hefty limb lying on the floor of the woods and another found a steel Coke can. We were on.

'Long about the fifth inning, me playing first base, Marion McCorkle cracked a hard line drive at me. I reached out for it, missed and it conked me square in the middle of the head. I went down like a sack of coal falling off a flat-bed truck and stayed there for about five minutes, dead, my pals must have thought. Minutes later, I shook my head, opened my eyes and looked up at a whole group of 10-year-olds just bawling, thinking I was off into that baseball game in the sky. It hurt like the dickens where that knot was raised.

*

The games didn't stop with the end of childhood. But they had to stop eventually, at least in their previous form.

If there's anything good about advancing age—and we're stretching to use the word "good"—it's that those experiencing it don't have to play in any more family holiday basketball games.

It's been years since one of my younger relations, or even my older brother, Sandy, sought me out to complete a team. This has none of the potential to be as traumatic as being the last kid picked at recess: my history in these games leads to relief at being ignored.

The last time I played—and let me emphasize that it was the very last time—I wound up unable to raise either of my arms above my shoulders for 18 months and I'm still fighting the residual dull ache in both my shoulders. That piles on top of injuries to both knees, a tooth knocked loose, what I thought was a broken nose (it would have been my fourth), toes crushed by huge-footed nephews, lingering shots to the solar plexus, a jaw that still doesn't open right and a hearing loss.

My favorite ex-wife told me once that it looked like I was trying on old age before I reached it.

These games started innocently enough, before my nephews and my own children were born. They were a way to keep from fighting inside the house when we gathered at Mom's for Christmas or Thanksgiving with our young families. We'd always been a competitive bunch—ritualistic torture by brother is a form of competition, Sandy insists—and the games, at first, just released steam from that pot.

As we all got older and had to go to work the next day, the game changed from football to basketball. Most of the guys in my family had been athletes at one level or another and the sons and nephews developed that way, too. The games were interesting, until the nephews got bigger and the older brothers got meaner.

Nephews Chuck and Tim, especially, were hard to get by, both of them going about 260 pounds and hovering over me by what felt like a foot. I damaged my shoulders one sunny November afternoon, full of comfort food and aggression, when Chuck turned around. That's all he did: turn around. The wake from his movement bounced me off the garage door and onto the pavement. I sat there for a good minute, disbelieving. There was this searing pain in my shoulders and a worse pain in my ego, which technically, I think, was inflamed.

Maybe worse than the injuries was the ridicule. "Get up, old man," said Sandy, who's older than me. "Are you OK?" delicately asked my sister-in-law, Jackie, implying I couldn't take it. "Quit whining and play," said nephew Jason, a hotshot who hated interruption. "I think he's done," said Chuck, Tim nodding in agreement. "Stick a fork in him. Hahahahahahahahah!"

Families don't tend to hold back when they see an opening and I'm stretched out in pain, hoping somebody has called 911 and here are seven guys hovering over me poking verbal sticks at me. Everybody laughs vigorously, but instead of offering me a hand or an ambulance, I hear my younger brother, Paul, say, "OK, it's 17-14; our ball. Jackie, take Danny's place," as they all turn toward the court and leave me to die.

**Posey's Funeral Home Pony League team about 1958. I'm on the
front row, second from the right. Jarhead is on top left. Jerk**

THE DAISY RED RYDER, MODEL 1939

It's difficult to say what the difference might have been. A sense of propriety, of right and wrong, perhaps. But when we shot each other, it wasn't for keeps. It wasn't even in anger. It was a game, like baseball, where there is a winner and a loser, but there wasn't finality in the shooting, as there appears to be occasionally in our confused and disjointed nation.

I ran across my old Daisy air rifle one day after the turn of the second millennium. It was about the same time that a couple of kids went mad and killed classmates in Colorado, Georgia and Kentucky.

When the Red Ryder was new, it was at the center of the world of play for me. The Daisy Red Ryder, Model 1939, BB gun faced down some ornery hombres, fearsome Nazis, screaming Comanches, wild-eyed Nips, big-hatted mobsters. It brought yelps from the kids in the neighborhood playing those parts, too; real yelps for real whelps, raised through double layers of blue jeans on the backs of thighs. This whole gang moved in and out of the trees to hide, ambush, kill or be killed for a few minutes at a time, until so many were dead that the game had to be stopped. Brutal stuff.

Padding—everything from extra clothes and folded newspapers, to throw pillows and woolen caps—was essential. Dying dramatically and playing dead for any period of more than 30 seconds became art forms.

Some of us grew up to continue the battle reluctantly in Vietnam with real guns and real bullets. And to die from them. Others became offended by war and by guns and fought non-killing battles against both. Some went to jail for believing in peace.

Looking back at the basic training in those sweltering, thick woods, there's nothing in that Daisy Red Ryder, Model 1939, that could possibly have predicted my pal Mike would go one way politically and I'd go the other. Mike shot me and I shot him with equal enthusiasm. We killed and we died and we spent the night with each other and we walked barefoot on the blistering South Carolina summer streets to the swimming pool and we played baseball and basketball until after dark. But we didn't think much about hurting anybody.

I don't know what our war taught us, but it certainly didn't encourage me to love the real thing or have anything like fondness for guns—except for that old Daisy, whose name suggests a kind of gentleness in its strength. It's the only gun I ever owned that actually shot a threatening projectile.

The power of the Daisy Red Ryder, Model 1939, was such that it ignored two pairs of thick pants and a double layer of underwear. It stung a right smart and it put deep dents into the two layers of screen wire covering the front of the football helmet I wore for war, sometimes sticking, always threatening to come through and create an international incident by putting my eye out. If my mother had known we were shooting BBs at each other, she would have pulled down all those pants and underwear layers and switched me blue. I'd have had to cut the switch.

None of Mom's anger, though, would have had political overtones. It would have been an overprotective mother's instinct, hanging on the standard wisdom that the only function of a BB gun was to shoot the eyes out of young children.

The only mother I ever knew who challenged that assumption was my Aunt Nell, who could outshoot any of us and whose eldest, Sonny, was allowed to shoot his Red Ryder gun *in the yard*, sometimes in Coke bottle cap competition with Aunt Nell, who always won.

Sonny didn't grow up to kill anybody in anger, either, though he matured between wars he might have fought had there been an opportunity.

The attraction of that old Daisy has confused me for a nearly half a century. I don't like guns and don't want them around, but there's something about the Daisy Red Ryder that exempts it from being a gun. It was hefty, sleek, smooth, balanced and thumped back at me in recoil when I pulled the trigger. I could see the BB speeding toward its target and could celebrate its collision, not so far removed from shooting a basketball, hitting a baseball, kicking a football.

Maybe the appeal lies in those hot days in the woods, looking down from my kudzu-covered perch up that pine tree, waiting for Mike Graybill to get in range so I could hear him holler when I put one in his butt.

In 1968, I was a lost soul: 22 years old, divorced, drinking,
searching for something that wasn't there. I wasn't so much
angry, as this photo suggests, as I was confused and rudderless

PART II:
GROWING UP

RAISIN' HELL

When some of the older guys, clustered in front of their lockers on the main hall at the high school, stood and talked just above a whisper about "raising hell last night," I didn't have much of an idea what that meant until a small bunch of us and a big bunch of them raised hell one early summer evening when I was 15.

Up to that point, "raising hell" had been a vague concept. I thought maybe it included the BB gun wars we kids had when I was 10 and 11. Our mothers would have killed us. It certainly included the time Mike Graybill and I set the woods on fire up near his house when we sneaked off to smoke rabbit tobacco, a nasty, feathery, sweet little gray plant that you could smoke or chew. I knew that was "raising hell" because a cop came to the door the day after the fire and I was terrified that I was going to jail. He shook his finger in my face and told me so.

I think that maybe circling the barely post-pubescent girls sitting along the side of the public pool—Panic Pond, built at the time of the fall of the stock market in 1929, hence "Panic"—trying to look down their bathing suits and see what was making that protrusion in the front when we were 10 or 11 might have qualified with the asterisk that we were green and without any understanding of how sex works, but were feeling these strange urges. The night Bebe Lang and I stole this 150-pound, 6 ½-foot tall floor fan from a mausoleum, only to drop it by the side of the road 30 minutes later when we found out we didn't know what to do with it, was certainly "raising hell" because it involved a crime, suspense and a cover-up.

The night we first raised hell as part of a plan was another one of those Friday nights when Bobby Payne—"Gut," we called him because of a slight paunch—had the little boxy, pale blue English Ford, the one with the sharp metal spur on the wheel-well that everybody who got into the back seat from the left side tore his pants on. When I got in that night—and tore my pants—I was the last into the car, and we were going somewhere, but nobody had any idea where. "Let's go over to Big Island," said Grady Martin.

"What's going on there?" Bobby asked.

"I dunno," said Grady.

"How 'bout nuthin'?" Bobby said. "There's not even a stop light in Big Island. I don't know what you're thinking."

"There's a big fraternity party at the Julian Smith Casino in Augusta, over near the lake," I said. "My dad used to do the food for these things and he said there would be about 500 teenagers from the three Augusta high schools there. They'll have a band, probably one of those college bands." High school fraternities were standard in the two big public and one small Catholic high schools in Augusta. We didn't have fraternities at North Augusta High because our students were already snooty and clannish and didn't need to be taught that.

"Yeah," said Grady, "and they'll have a cover charge that'll take my allowance for a month. How 'bout Fleming Teen Town? They got a band, too, and all those girls from Butler High School go over there. There's some mighty fine women in that crowd." Women. Yeah. Big shots, us.

This went on for a while, arguing back and forth, suggestions and refusals. Finally, from beside me in the back seat, Fuzzy ("Don't call me Johnny") Floyd, who had been quiet the entire time, said, "Let's hit the casino. I know a way to get in and we won't have to pay cover."

Fuzzy'd been around a while longer than the rest of us and we all knew he had a flair for the dramatic. I think he'd failed some subjects and was in most of our classes, even though he was 16 and should have been a year ahead. Bobby, me and Grady were all 15—kids could get a full driver's license at the time in South Carolina, so Bobby was driving legally—and were only just beginning to find our social legs. None of us'd had any dates to speak of, especially me, since I didn't have a car, or any money, or any idea how to go about asking a girl out.

North Augusta was a snotty little upper-middle-class town where fathers were engineers at the Savannah River Nuclear Plant (people, in their South Carolina accents, called it the "bum plant"), and mothers were of the stay-at-home-and-play-bridge variety. The four of us didn't scratch that society. We were at various points along the downwardly mobile: Grady and Fuzzy didn't have fathers at home because of divorces, which was unusual in 1962. Bobby had two parents at home. His dad who sold insurance or did something like that, and the family was the closest to the economic norm. I was farthest away, my father having died in 1960 and all of us—five kids left at home—living on what Mom could scrape together, plus Dad's tiny Social Security check.

People seemed to like all of us, but we weren't part of their social order. So we went across the Savannah River into Georgia—Augusta, home of James Brown, Otis Redding, Larry Jon Wilson, Terri Gibbs, The Masters, Geechees, sandspurs, fleas, humidity—and made friends there. We liked it in Augusta where people were more like us. There was a certain forbidden fruit element to it, especially when the kids at North Augusta High School, home of the Yellow Jackets, the 1962 state AA football champions, found out that we'd been socializing with their blood enemies.

We had hung out at Fleming Teen Town through most of the spring, after one of the girls invited Grady over back during basketball season after a game. He'd dragged us along to protect him, and we'd learned some of the rudiments of dancing—I was pretty good at the Twist ("Come on Baby, let's do the Twist...") and could get by with the Frug, Swim, Watusi, Pony and a couple of others. None of us drank yet—it just hadn't come up—so that particular social lubricant and dance capability expander had not yet entered into our arsenal of courting tools.

Grady was a drummer of some reputation, later playing professionally. He was also the first of us to recognize the value in what we'd later call "soul music." Listening to Black music was another reason for other kids to wonder about us. Fuzzy was a good enough natural athlete to flow nicely in any crowd. Bobby did OK, but was more self-conscious than the rest of us, even though he was the guy with the car.

The Julian Smith Casino, sitting above Lake Olmstead, was the centerpiece building in one of the best parks in Augusta. It was a gray building with a large turret near the corner and a number of palladium windows across the front that opened out toward the lake. People hung out there at night and looked at the lights. The casino was then—and is now—The Place for a Big Party in Augusta.

Bobby pulled the English Ford, a car not much bigger than a VW Bug, into what was a piece of a parking space and we squeezed out the doors, pushing them up against the cars on either side of us. I tore my pants again. "Bobby, you ever going to get this dang thing fixed?" I pleaded rhetorically.

"No," he said. "I don't ride back there. You fix it."

There were maybe 50 young people, dressed nicely, milling in the parking lot, some leaning against cars smoking or taking sips from paper bags, some sitting in the back seats of cars, usually in pairs and usually pretty close, as we eased our way through small groups and car radios—blaring Dion's "Wanderer" and Booker T's "Green Onions," Gene Chandler's "Duke of Earl," Bruce Channel's "Hey Baby" and Acker Bilk's (Acker Bilk?) "Stranger on the Shore," a blazing cacophony—trying not to draw attention.

"Come on around this way," said Fuzzy in a loud whisper, pointing toward the back of the building. We heard the thump of an electric bass from inside and we could almost recognize tunes occasionally.

Fuzzy stopped and gathered the three of us around him. "OK," he said, "here's the plan: Every time the band stops, people mill around for a few seconds, change partners, go get something to drink and stuff. There's a lot of moving around. So what we're going to do is climb through the bathroom window and when the music stops, we run out onto the dance floor and pair up with a girl as the next song starts. Just get next to somebody and start dancing. Nobody'll ever know where we came from if they notice us at all."

I'd never before heard Fuzzy say that many words at once, but it all sounded easy and clearly logical to the three of us who'd never been inside Julian Smith Casino, never been to a fraternity party, never danced to a band of college boys wearing coats and ties, never been around kids our age who were drinking, never done a whole lot of stuff we were getting ready to do.

Testosterone was mixing evenly with endorphins and adrenaline at the moment I got on my knees and one-by-one the others stepped on my back and climbed into the window. Fuzzy reached a hand out for me and pulled me in. I flipped into the low-lit bathroom, turning a complete somersault and landing on my feet in the middle of about 25 boys. All of whom had the same idea we had.

The band was banging out the final chords of the "Peppermint Twist" and two dozen teenaged boys crowded together at the bathroom door. When the last note was struck, the door flung open and we stormed the dance floor like Marines hitting the beach. I landed next to Christine Cash, a tall, willowy, pretty girl with shoulder-length black hair—she looked like a live Veronica from "Archie"—whom I knew from Fleming Teen Town. Bobby glommed onto blue-eyed, stacked Alice Peterson, a sophomore at Richmond Academy and another Teen Town regular, who danced a great Pony. Fuzzy and Grady disappeared (Grady had gone straight to the bandstand to watch the drummer, I discovered later, and Fuzzy wound up in a corner with a dazzling blonde, making out). At the same second Christine recognized me and smiled, the band hit the first notes of Joey Dee's "Shout, Part I" and we had arrived as bona fide hell-raisers, dancing with exotic girls from other schools.

During the dance, there were small, well, "skirmishes" for want of a better word, all over the dance floor and by the time "Shout, Part I" was over, a bunch of the guys from the bathroom mob scene had been briskly escorted out the door. When one of the big, crew-cut bouncer types stopped Christine and me and asked who I was, she batted those foot-long eyelashes and said, "He's with me." I grew a foot and a half in that second.

About an hour later, Christine and I were in the back seat of a big, black, 1962 Mercury out in the parking lot, listening to Mary Wells sing "The One Who Really Loves You." She had taken me by the hand after an especially warm, close slow dance and led me out of the building to the car. We climbed in and sat in silence for long moments. I had no idea what I was doing, which was nothing. Christine began talking just above a whisper in that husky, sexy voice of hers and I thought maybe I should kiss her, but I didn't know how to go about it, whether to just jump right in or maybe slip an arm up over the back of the seat and slowly slide toward her first. So, what I did was still mostly nothing.

"What you guys did was really funny and really courageous," she said, sliding slightly closer, her hip touching mine and a small breast brushing my upper arm as she turned toward me. The soft touches riveted my attention. Her breast felt huge and naked and the sensation between my legs was unmistakable. Did I dare touch her, kiss her, talk to her? No, not yet. Just another minute.

"When I saw you coming out of the bathroom in that group, I was so surprised. I never expected anything like that and when you stopped in front of me …"

"Would you like to wear my letter jacket?" I said.

"I couldn't," she said. "The kids at school would tear it to pieces, but if you have a pin…"

I didn't have a pin. I didn't have words. They wouldn't come. I was stuck.

"Mostly nothing" kept adding up until about 20 minutes into our promising moment, Christine abruptly said, "Danny, let's go back inside and dance some more" and so we did, my brief sexual awakening abruptly put back to sleep. I knew I'd missed my first best opportunity, but I didn't know what else to do but tag along behind her, savoring the partial triumphs of being in the car with her—and what the guys would think of that—and knowing that "raising hell" earlier had caught her attention.

"Play 'Bobby's Girl,'" I screamed as we reached the dance floor again, temporarily forgetting my setback and feeling fully licensed as a teenage desperado. Bobby smacked me on the back of the head.

Next morning, as I responded to the smells of frying bacon and baking biscuits, wobbling half asleep into the kitchen, prying my eyes open as I went, Mom greeted me with a cup of mostly cream and sugar coffee and said, "Well, hotshot, how was the dance?" How'd she know? She always knew. Always. Dangdest thing I ever saw.

"What dance?" I asked, knowing she knew I was lying and she knowing I knew.

"Leave your pants on the sewing machine and I'll fix them today," she said.

The Julian Smith Casino is still a destination in Augusta

**My mom's favorite picture of Dad;
he was a senior cadet at Virginia Tech
in 1933, the year they met**

DADDY DIES

Sandy stood at my bedroom door looking at me with a combination of challenge and concern. "Daddy died last night," he said without emotion. "Doctor told Mama yesterday Daddy wouldn't make it through the night, and he didn't. You better get up and come on downstairs."

I was sitting upright, half covered, rubbing my eyes. "Where's Mama? She alright?" I said.

"She's fine. You know Mama. Just get your clothes on and come on down."

    *

I didn't find out until much later when Mom pulled me aside and whispered that Dad officially had been poisoned. Mom told everybody else that Dad's vital organs had finally given in to his alcoholism and that was true as far as she went. I guess she didn't want to start a bunch of speculation. Dad had actually been poisoned by a batch of bad moonshine he had picked up on one of his drunken trips to East Tennessee a few months earlier.

Years later, Sandy called me in Roanoke from Oak Ridge and breathlessly asked, "Did you know Dad was poisoned?"

When I said, "Yeah, I knew that," there was silence on his end of the phone for an unpleasant moment. "How'd you know? Why didn't you tell anybody?"

"I found out when I was 13, right after he died," I said. "Mom told me and said not to tell anybody else, so I just forgot it. Hearing you say it is the first time I've thought about it since then."

*

Dad was an on-again, off-again practicing alcoholic throughout his marriage to Mom. I suspect he picked up drinking in college, since he was from a pretty straight-laced German-Irish Christian family (his father died on the way to church), and I believe the alcoholism amplified when he was stationed in Bremerton, Ore., as the captain in charge of a munitions depot during World War II. I can't imagine a guy who wanted to be a career soldier being stationed in a small town, running something like a munitions depot during a time of war and not spending a lot of time drinking.

Mom suffered it all, though rarely quietly. She complained about Dad for years, especially to us kids. He had left her for long periods—during the war, and afterwards when he'd get an urge to move to another town and he'd take off looking for work—and she'd been so desperate at times that she farmed out the three oldest children, Buck to Aunt Nell in the mountains of North Carolina and Patti and Judy to families in Johnson City who didn't have kids and thought the little Smith girls were precious.

Patti never came back and was all but officially adopted by her family, the Martins. It was good for her, though, because she lived a normal middle class life and managed to get a college education and solid respectability out of her life. She was greatly disappointed later when the Martins died without having written a will. Mr. Martin meant to, but just didn't get around to it. She later said, "The Martins gave me so much love and contributed [so significantly] to my self esteem that I can never begrudge the lack of inheritance."

Buck got pretty much the same treatment at Aunt Nell's comfortable home in Avery County, N.C., where a good home with good people—my mother grew up in that house—protected him from our poverty. Judy stayed a while with her family, the Lacys, but, always the rebel, came home. Judy was a big help to Mom, but she got married at 16 to a guy who would work in one of South Carolina's textile factories for the rest of his life. She had a big family and finally divorced the jerk when in her middle years, marrying a nice guy named Fred. Good old Fred.

The distribution of kids across the countryside still left Mom with a gang of us, little money and no training even if she could have left us for a job. I always had the impression Dad was not exactly punctual about sending money to us when he was gone, though Mom never said one way or the other.

Dad was a diabetic and after World War II, when he had decided to stay in the Army as a career move (he was on the verge of being elevated to major), the diabetes was discovered and papers were being prepared to muster him out on a medical discharge. He was devastated and Mom said he simply disappeared for a year. The Army was not amused and sent out people looking for him.

"They found him in a motel room and stormed in with a full squad of MPs," Mom told me, grinning widely in retrospect. "Can you imagine anybody pointing a gun at your daddy?" As I've said, Mom saw the humor in everything.

Dad spent a year in Leavenworth Federal Prison and his prospects for employment in the judgmental 1940s and 1950s (The Shame Decade) were significantly diminished, even though he had a rare college degree—business administration, dean's list—and was role-model smart. He settled on restaurant work because people rarely asked questions in that line, and he liked to cook and be around food. I remember few times when I didn't see him dressed in restaurant whites, almost like a nurse, and those times were on Monday nights during that several years when he went to an AA meeting, dressed in his only suit.

Dad was, indeed, an even-tempered, gentle soul, probably a lot more intellectual than we kids knew. He read a book a day after work—a lot of Zane Grey, but a book a day is a book a day, even if it's a comic book—and the physicians who frequented the restaurant he ran were forever asking him for information and advice (and not just about sports as Mom said).

*

Dad drove a 1946 Dodge coupe, powder blue and white, impressively rounded fenders and a spotlight on the driver's side. It had been a police car at one point in its life and I always loved that old car—dreaming of its desperate chases of outlaws—though at the time I fluctuated between pride at its pedigree and shame at its age.

The Dodge was about 10 years old when Dad bought it for, I think, $100—which seemed to be the standard for cars he drove. He put a dollar's worth of gas in the car every Monday and drove it to work at the restaurant, across the Savannah River in Augusta seven days on that. Sometimes he took us to Dairy Queen on Sunday afternoon—after a fried chicken picnic at Julian Smith Park—on what was left of that four or five gallons of gas. (We ate fried chicken on Sunday afternoon 52 weeks a year, no matter what else was happening in God's world.)

That Dodge had a passenger-side door that sometimes swung open unexpectedly when Dad made right turns. He had developed a conditioned reflex: the minute the door started to open, his hand shot across the seat and grabbed whichever kid was there and held him in place until the car could be stopped and the door closed again. It was a smooth, practiced, panic-free move. Dad had this coolness about him that I always thought

**Dad in the
Army in 1942**

was steady and stable. I trusted him and I think all the other kids did, too. Mom could be a little nutty, but Dad was like that big old tree in the back yard, the one we climbed and built forts and houses in.

Once in a while we piled into the Dodge and headed off for the drive-in movies, the only kind of movie we could afford to go to together, since a car-load got in for the price of the driver. Mom boiled or roasted a big bag of peanuts—that would be a grocery bag, just like the one Dad took to baseball games—and we got to the theater at dusk so the kids could play on the swings and slides. Then we'd sit on the still-warm hood and watch some of the movie, most often something Mom wanted to see like "The Three Faces of Eve" (based on a book by her shrink, a guy named Thigpen) or one of Dad's Big Westerns of John Ford and Frankie Laine, say, "Red River" or "Shane." Me and the other kids climbed into the back seat and went to sleep when we couldn't sit up any longer. Sometimes we'd watch the teenaged daters fog up their windows and wallow in each other.

*

About a year before Dad died, we finally moved back to the mountains of North Carolina where Mom longed to be for the entire 11 years we lived in South Carolina, a hellishly hot, bug-infested place she hated. But dad got sick shortly after we moved back to Asheville and they both knew

they'd be safer to pull up stakes again and trudge back to North Augusta. Dad's friends were there and some of them were doctors who could take care of him.

But he died—the last time I saw him, he was a 90-pound shadow of his 210-pound self, breathing with difficulty in an iron lung, pale and sallow—and we were stuck in what Mom considered perdition for another two years, living from one tiny Social Security check to the next, taking charity, asking for

Mom, Paul, Becky about the time Dad died

loans, missing meals, watching as the gas man, the electric man, the water man, the phone man, showed up to shut off service periodically. We often came home from school and were greeted with a fire in the fireplace, the first sign the heat was off. "We're camping tonight," Mom would say cheerfully.

Once a group of Sandy's friends dropped by unexpectedly and we were all huddled in blankets in front of the fire. Sandy was mortified that he'd been found out. But the friends didn't understand we were doing what we had to do. They thought we were camping in the house because it was fun. I don't know that they ever understood how wrong they were, because I doubt if the concept that we were poor registered with them.

The house we lived in when Dad died—we called it The Big House— was a huge old Spanish home, probably 100 years old, at the top of the hill on the main street in North Augusta, across the street from Channel 13, the local TV station. It was enormous: five bedrooms, three baths, two stairways, a cavernous living room, dining room and entry hall, oak fixtures, chandeliers, hardwood floors and in the bathroom rich tile. There were fireplaces in just about every room and it was surrounded by a large, nicely landscaped front yard and a back yard that had a long grape vine on a trellis leading from just off the back porch to the back-back yard. In that back-back were fig and plum trees. We ate the plums and Concord grapes and threw the figs at each other during war games because we didn't know what else to do with them.

It was a wonderful place where we played football on the front lawn and climbed on the grape arbor. There was even a small house that had been servants' quarters, though a grumpy old couple lived there and didn't like us kids, so we stayed away from them when we weren't subverting their quiet comfort. I had no idea how we afforded this luxurious home, though I knew the rent was low. Could have been one of Dad's doctor pals giving us a break with a house he owned; I just don't know. Heat bills alone could easily have broken us, even with Dad alive and working.

Sandy, Paul, David and Becky watch TV at the Big House

We stayed there for a while after Dad died, but finally had to move because we couldn't pay the rent, low as it was. Moving was something we did periodically, in any case. Mom was always on the lookout for a house that would hold us all and be cheap, knowing that eventually we wouldn't have enough money to stay where we were and we'd be asked to leave. Sandy tells the story about coming home for a visit from college late at night once and finding a note on the front door reading, "We're four houses up. Door unlocked."

I don't know why Mom never asked us to go to work, or even encouraged it. I said several times that I wanted to work, but she'd say, "You just go to school and don't worry about working for a while, young man. I'll take care of it."

Paul and Becky, the youngest kids, eventually dropped out of school, Paul in the 9th grade, Becky in the 10th. They didn't want to go and Mom didn't have the strength to make them. Sandy was a star football and basketball player at the high school, and that opened opportunities for him. Buck, Patti and Judy were grown and gone away; David was slightly retarded and there was no option but to simply encourage him and teach him what could be taught (he worked at a bakery for several years before killing himself—the cops said suicide, but it probably was an unfortunate accident—at 24) and I struggled along, going to school, playing a little football, trying to make a few friends and pass my classes.

The poverty resulting from Dad's death—we were poor when he was alive, but that intensified without his income and he had left us nothing; his funeral was paid for by some of his friends—was difficult on a number of levels. For me, the poverty was a constant source of humiliation. The other kids and I got free lunches at school, for example, and each Monday, the teacher would call us to the front of the class first thing in the morning to get our lunch tickets. (The high school football coach was Sandy's homeroom teacher and Coach Calley Gault had enough common courtesy and grace to hand out the tickets quietly.) My clothes weren't what the other kids wore and often I didn't have money for school fees, that fact being announced to the class as the teacher, in essence, told my classmates that I was a charity case. The pain was worse than the hunger we sometimes felt because we knew Mom would come up with something for the hunger, but that we couldn't cure people's notions of us as trash.

My year-older brother David's burden was probably the worst. He was only slightly "retarded," and I have no idea how that designation was reached since he wasn't Mongoloid and his learning deficiencies weren't obvious. He was placed in "special" classes ("I'm not retarded," he often bellowed. "I hate being in this class") and the "normal" kids made fun of him.

There is little wonder he ultimately killed himself, though it took a while. (David had a habit of staying up late watching TV around the time of his death. He'd often act out something from what he'd watched the night before and Mom speculated that he'd seen somebody hang himself the night he died.)

Mom enjoyed David, often using that wicked, irreverent sense of humor of hers at his expense, but coming from her it was not hurtful and he enjoyed her jokes. I remember once, she put down the telephone after a call from the elementary school, and stood in utter horror. "David told the teacher I stabbed him," she deadpanned, not knowing whether to be mortified or falling on the floor from laughter. His teacher had asked David about the small bandage on his hand and he'd told of the "stabbing."

Actually, he had been hovering around Mom while she was sewing some pants, annoying and distracting her and she had reached out and lightly hit his hand with a pair of scissors, drawing a tiny amount of blood. Finally, Mom burst into laughter at the absurdity of it. Later, she tapped him over the head with a plate because he was annoying her while she cooked supper, the plate broke and he told the teacher that, too. What they must have thought of Mom.

*

I don't remember crying when Dad died. We knew it was coming and I guess we were exhausted from worry when it finally did. I cried about it for the first time when I was 44, 31 years later. And, God's truth, I don't know what brought that on. One day I just started crying and couldn't stop.

The Big House is where we lived when Dad died. It was quite a place

THE LANGUAGE
OF THE SEWER

Vulgar language is not hereditary, a conclusion I reached after only 59 years, some of which—during the early part—had been lived without cuss words and without any noticeable damage for their lack.

I matured at a time and in an industry where the cultural norm included the rawest and loudest forms of crude expression in what was mostly a boys club. The women in news most often hid out in the "Society" offices, half-a-building removed, and the daily grind newswomen, who wouldn't be caught near the women's department, were among our saltiest, former WACs or Army nurses or oil wildcatters. There was a distinct difference in those two types of women, as clear as the beats they covered. On the one hand there were the pinky-pointing, white glove and small hat-wearing, slender, prim women whose most offensive expletive was, "Oh, my."

The babes in the newsroom dressed more in the spirit of the street beat with minimal makeup (mostly a touch of lipstick at the last minute), loose, sometimes wrinkled skirts and pants, dull colors, plain blouses open at the throat, no hats, hair to their shoulders or shorter, sensible shoes. Their language mirrored ours, lots of "hell," "damn," "shit," an occasional "fuck" and a constant flow of "sumbitch" when talking about work. There were no women in sports.

*

My dad never cussed about anything. You knew he was on the verge of exploding if he said, "Oh, durn!" That was as far over the edge as he'd get and when Dad said "durn" you might want to give him a broad berth, your full attention or else find a close exit, whichever could be accomplished first.

Dad said "durn" the time he whipped me—the only time. I'd snapped back something nasty at Mom, and Dad simply didn't want that to be done. So he popped me one on the butt. It didn't hurt nearly as much as Mom's "cut me a switch and don't make it a willow" moments. She'd lay it on and sometimes it did, indeed, sting pretty good.

It was the subtlety, the total unexpectedness of Dad's not very expletive-like expletive, that got to me. I guess that's what it was about with his Cuss-Free Zone language.

Dad, a strapping former college football player, Army officer and man's man, once told me that an educated man didn't need to cuss. The smart guy could cut you to ribbons "using the language God gave him." Cussing, he said, "is a sign of a lack of education," a sign of being "common." God forbid. Common. Whoa.

Mom used "common" like Mike Graybill's dad used "sumbich" and Dad rarely had cause to call anybody anything as awful as "sumbich." "That man's just common," Mom would say about Mike's dad after hearing him ask her, "How's that old sumbich George?" meaning my dad.

I once said "durn"—after coming to the conclusion that it was OK because Dad said it sometimes—and she whipped me. "That's going too far, young man. You're lucky I don't wash your mouth out with soap," she cautioned.

"But Mama," I pleaded, "Daddy said 'durn' yesterday" to which she replied with yet another switching for saying "durn" again.

"Your daddy can say anything he wants to say, Mr. Big Stuff," Mom said, "but you can't!"

I didn't think it was fair, but I wasn't in a position to sue.

I must have been all the way out of high school and into "real life" as the high school counselors used to say (as in, "when you get out into real life …") before I said anything stronger than "dad-blame" on a regular basis. There were one or two uncharacteristic outbursts—notably during a football injury when I strung together some surprising observations—but nothing consistent.

I grew up professionally in newsrooms, heavily male, more like locker rooms in the early days before women's communication skills overcame men's natural crudeness and added a civilizing influence. My first few years in the business, there were three requirements beyond knowing the rudiments of English: One had to smoke, drink copious amounts of coffee (during work, booze afterwards) and cuss, performing all three without regard for the circumstance of the moment. Newsrooms often resembled and sounded like bars, heavy smoke hanging and people yelling at each other with colorful vulgarities. Some, truth be known, had started happy hour before coming to work in the late afternoon, as well. The cussing and smoking were not just accepted; they was part of the ambiance of the craft, part of the legend. The drinking was often ignored, rarely punished.

I took these new skills home: my daughter's first word was "shit." She smilingly called her grandmother "son-of-a-bitch" before she was 3. Mom wasn't happy about that, as you might imagine.

The first time I went down with a knee injury as a 15-year-old in a junior varsity football game, I blurted, "damn, damn, double-damn, triple-damn, shit!" I sat there on the ground all by myself—the play had gone about 30 yards up field, and both teams with it—the stadium deep forest silent, all eyes on me, mortified, not that I'd destroyed any pro football or knee-wear modeling future. They were stunned because I had broken that cussing taboo with an Olympic Gold performance. The verbal *faux pas* had so astonished this prudish little community that I could hear a murmur begin circulating, not about whether I'd live, but denying having heard my outburst. "He couldn't have said what we heard him say," I heard a blonde cheerleader standing about 10 yards from me whisper to another blonde cheerleader, both wearing the opponent's orange and black.

(These were the same two cheerleaders who had screamed, "Oh, shit!" like they were being assaulted when I got tackled close to them about half a quarter earlier and the guy who tackled me pulled my pants down to my knees. I wasn't wearing underwear, just a jock, so my shiny white butt gleamed. The pants were new and the company that made them had sent college sizes, which didn't fit. Most of the guys had taped theirs on. I hadn't and so they came off. It was a tough night for these two delicate flowers.)

When the trainer got to me as I lay on the ground helpless, my knee swelling and so mad I was still muttering, he said, "What were you thinking, Smith? Don't you know there are decent people here and that they have children with them?"

"Uh, no, sir," I said, embarrassed, "I wadn't thinking about much except that I went left and my knee went right and it hurt a whole lot more than you know."

"That's no excuse for bad manners or for cussing," he directed. "You'll not see the field again, if I have anything to do with it."

He didn't have much to do with it and I saw the field about 15 minutes later, my knee tightly taped. He got his point across, though, when, after the game he came over and ripped the tape off my knee, which hadn't been shaved.

I didn't cuss again for maybe three years, when I was about 18. That was when the boys I hung out with—just about the same time I began working at the Asheville Citizen's sports department—began to make a big deal of the fact that I said "durn" instead of "damn" and that they'd never heard me say so much as "hell."

"You weird?" my buddy Coot once asked me, straight up, as if to inquire about my sexual preferences. That sealed the future of discourse for me: "Hell, no, I ain't *weird* and damn you for asking," I said, as I embarked upon a journey of uninterrupted life in language's sewers that my by-then-dead-five-years dad would have reviled in utter disgust.

About 15 years after Coot's rhetorical question, I wrote a feature story for The Roanoke Times about cussing and learned that Americans and their "damns," "hells," "shits" and the like were considered unsophisticated pikers in the world of cussing—or "cursing" as the more refined called it. A real curse left the receiver humiliated or embarrassed, not just mad and wanting to scream something simple-minded back.

"Fuck you!" has a certain power when used sparingly or unexpectedly (say when The Church Lady says it) but when has it been used sparingly by me or anybody else over the years? It's as common as "Whassup?"

There are alternatives, some of them novel, if difficult to pronounce. How about something like these little Gaelic marvels?

Go n–ithe an cat thú, is go n–ithe an diabhal an cat (May the cat eat you, and may the devil eat the cat);

Go lagaí galar tógálach do chroí (May an infectious disease weaken your heart);

Has a certain *joie de vivre*? Dad would have approved.

The dormer of the front of Little Boys cabin at Grandfather Home for Children is where I lived during my senior year of high school

THE HOME

At the end of the school year in 1963, my junior year of high school and my 16th year of life, we moved back to Asheville from the Augusta suburb where I'd grown up.

It was starting to look like we were confused about where we wanted to live because we had moved from North Augusta, S.C., to Asheville, back to North Augusta and then, finally, back to Asheville within a period of about three years.

We had lived in Asheville briefly when I was in junior high, but Dad got sick and we needed some people around us who could help with that, so we returned to North Augusta, Mom hating every minute of it. She had never liked South Carolina because of the heat, the bugs, the lack of mountains and cool nights. It was almost a consuming fact of her life after a while. She simply hated this place and there was nothing that would make her change her mind, which Dad had tried to do for years.

After Dad died, we stayed on in North Augusta for as long as she could take it, but she'd finally had all of South Carolina that she could stand and we returned to Asheville, knowing nobody, having nothing in North Carolina, save Mom's good memories of her home.

I was thoroughly displaced, lonely and frustrated, so I asked Mom if I could visit Aunt Nell in Cranberry for the summer. Cranberry is a village in Avery County about 80 miles north of Asheville in what Western North Carolinians call the "high country" subdivision of the Blue Ridge Mountains. It is near Mount Mitchell, the highest mountain in the eastern United States, and the base altitude is something higher than a mile.

My oldest brother, Buck, had grown up with Aunt Nell and her family and even Mom had lived with them when she was young. My brother Sandy had visited Cranberry and loved it.

I believed it would be better than Asheville, where I knew I would struggle through the summer and be lost in its huge high school, Lee Edwards High, which was at least twice the size of the schools I was accustomed to. I would be nothing, nobody there.

Mom was reluctant, but my pleading led her to write Aunt Nell and ask and, of course, my sainted aunt, being what one refers to as a "good Christian woman" in the best sense, said sure, send him on.

Cranberry had 62 families, two general stores, a diner, a high school, a gas station and a church, where Aunt Nell was a deacon, something rare, I was told. The village had been a cranberry bog long ago, but an iron mine across the street from Aunt Nell—where my grandfather, William McCurry, and an uncle, Ethmon, had worked—became the center of commerce. A small-gauge train—later Tweetsie, the tourist attraction in Blowing Rock—ran from the mine, behind Aunt Nell's house and on down to Elizabethton, Tenn., in one direction and Marion, N.C., in the other, to deliver ore.

Aunt Nell was the postmistress, a job with a lot of status and not a lot of responsibility. She was the classic image of the village postmistress, a woman who'd let you know immediately when an important letter or package came for you and a person who knew and kept up with everybody. She was known throughout the county as a woman of great grace, compassion, generosity.

Aunt Nell had married my mother's favorite brother, Elbert—Eb, for whom I was named—but he had died a few years before I went up for the summer. Aunt Nell's beautiful daughter, Mary Elizabeth (MaryLiz to everybody), had died of leukemia at 24 a few years earlier. She had worked as a model and Aunt Nell doted on her because she was not only lovely, but she was a sweet, modest girl with a marvelous sense of humor. I was crazy about her and had only met her once. Aunt Nell's other kids, Sonny and Margaret, a sometimes folk singer, were grown and living in D.C. and West Virginia.

I never thought a lot about why Aunt Nell allowed me to spend the summer with her that year, but her own loneliness could have had something to do with it. She had been a mother for so long that I'm sure she missed it.

*

I found myself in the middle of something akin to paradise for a kid normally surrounded by siblings and poverty: a room of my own; mounds of good food; predictable electricity, phone service, gas and water; no competition from other kids; quiet if I wanted it. I was even introduced to people immediately and there was a lot to do, mostly outside, some of it having to do with chores, which I didn't mind, and some of it social. There were a surprising number of kids my age within a mile or two of Aunt Nell's house, some of them distant relatives of mine, and they liked to keep busy. One kid taught me to milk a cow. I went berry picking, and put up hay, getting into a nest of bees at one point and diving out of the loft of a barn into the back of the pickup we were throwing the hay into. I got poison ivy clearing brush in a cemetery and went swimming in the coldest creek I'd ever seen. I hiked through stingy-nettles and sudden rain storms, ate until I could no longer stand at church socials and worked out daily at the high school's football field, hoping against hope that I'd play again.

I especially liked hiking back to Hump Mountain, a high-grass, windswept bald spot on a mountain where wild horses once roamed (Mom told me the kids tried to ride them when she was a girl) and a few cattle still grazed. I once took Aunt Nell's octagon-barrel .22 rifle with me, ostensibly to hunt (something I knew nothing about). I came upon a fox, aimed the gun and pulled the trigger, but had left the safety on. It made me so mad that I shot a robin out of a tree and *that* upset me so much that I haven't fired a gun since.

Aunt Nell could fire one, though. We put bottle caps on a tree across the garden from the house, maybe 50 yards, and she could drill the middle of them shot after shot. I had trouble hitting the tree.

As the summer wore on, I began to fray Aunt Nell's nerves, I think. It was little things, stacked on top of each other. I was a teenager and, though I wasn't moody, I didn't always obey her requests immediately. I wanted to stay up later than she did. She didn't like rock 'n' roll music any time, but especially on Sundays and I had it playing almost all the time. I was lazier than she liked and was reluctant to do my share of the work. I ate a lot and I'm sure that put a strain on her budget. I didn't like going to her "holy roller" church and I told her. Frankly, saint or not, I don't think Aunt Nell was in the mood to raise another kid and she may have underestimated just how much of an intrusion a young virtual stranger would be when she said "yes" to my mother.

So, we sat down and talked about what to do next. Aunt Nell wanted to send me to Asheville and my mother; I wanted to stay and go to school at Cranberry High where I would know a few people and might even be able to play football. The school was small—the senior class had 78 people in it—and I was pretty sure I would be a good football player at that level, even though the orthopedist in North Augusta had told me not even to think about football after hurting my knee pretty dramatically.

We were at an impasse when Aunt Nell said, "What about The Home?"

"The Home?" I asked. "You mean Grandfather Home, the orphanage?"

"It's not an orphanage," she said. "It's more for displaced children and I think you qualify for that right now. It's a lovely place run by fine Christian people and you would be supervised."

I protested that I was not an orphan, not abused, not abandoned, not a Christian (Boy, did Aunt Nell love that announcement!), but she said my family's poverty and the fact that Mom had so many of us would likely open the door for me.

It did. A regal, white-haired, never-married woman everybody called Miss Anne, who had been at Grandfather Home for Children in Banner Elk for many years, showed me around and welcomed me after a long conversation with Aunt Nell, whom she knew and respected. I got the feeling that Aunt Nell called in an old debt in exchange for a little sanity and I was the beneficiary. I didn't know it then, but the cost for me to go there worked out to about $1 a day (according to the home's literature), so

Aunt Nell must have done something for Miss Ann that was especially valuable. A dollar doesn't sound like much, but that was $30 a month when rents were about $100 for a house.

*

Miss Anne personally showed me to what would be my quarters, a private room on the second floor of "Little Boys Cottage," where the youngest boys lived in what was hardly a cottage. There were seven campus buildings: administration offices, Big Boys, Little Boys, Big Girls, Little Girls, a small home that housed the youth director and his wife (smiling Christian youth workers of the type you know well), in addition to a gymnasium. The buildings were more lodge-like—native stone, exposed beams, hardwood floors, two stories—than cottages, with the exception of Big Boys, which was recently built, contemporary and made of wood, stone and glass, and they housed not only the children, but the paid "house parents" who were in charge of each building.

Grandfather Home's high school students, about 15 or so of us, caught the bus to Cranberry High, seven miles down a winding mountain road, before sunup and if any of us participated in after-school activities—football for me, later some basketball and the school play—we had to arrange for transportation back to the dorm, not always an easy thing to do since the whole county was poor and not many kids had cars.

*

The home was named for Grandfather Mountain, which was a few miles away and towered over everything. Geologists say the mountain was created 742 million years ago when the earth's plates slammed together and thrust skyward and that the mountain range that contains Grandfather— The Appalachians—is considerably older than the Himalayas, Rockies or other higher ranges. A 1962 U.S. Geological Survey estimated that some of the rock formations on Grandfather are 1.1 billion years old. When French botanist Andre Michaux climbed Grandfather in 1794, he proclaimed it the highest mountain in the eastern part of the United States, but he was wrong. Mt. Mitchell, in the Black Mountains about 40 miles south, is the tallest at 6,694, about 700 feet higher than Grandfather. Even Roan Mountain, over near Cranberry and an extension of The Hump, which you can see from Grandfather, is about 300 feet higher.

Time wears everything out, though, and this old mountain—it looks like a grandpa's face, lying in repose—has become a tourist haven.

Grandfather Home was founded in 1914 as an orphanage by Rev. Edward Tufts, a Presbyterian minister. He converted a farmhouse belonging to Lees-McRae Institute—Lees-McRae College since 1931. The Home, college and Grace/Canon Memorial Hospital (where I later had knee surgery) were all under the Presbytery.

An old man and old lady—whose names I don't recall, but we called them "Mom" and "Pop"—ran "Little Boys" and they were a kindly sort, who chose to leave me alone. I had a room whose main feature was a slope-roofed dormer that I liked a lot. Private room, left alone. A teenager's dream.

Most of the kids slept in military-style group dormitory rooms. We got up about 6 o'clock each morning and walked over to the administration building where the dining room was. Several of the "Big Girls" came down the hill each morning to prepare breakfast and some of the boys served the meals. I don't think boys were allowed to cook. Each Sunday, we had to go to church and we had vespers—required—twice a week. We also had a huge, wonderful lunch that I anticipated each week.

*

There was rarely a problem for me at the home. I lived separately from the other boys in my loft room, was a senior in high school and, thus, older, and, frankly, I felt apart from them. One Saturday night, though, when the old couple that oversaw Little Boys was out of town for the weekend and I was ostensibly in charge, I went downstairs to tell the boys to bathe and get ready to go to bed, and to help the smallest ones, who needed it, get their teeth brushed and into their pajamas. Most of the kids recognized that I had some authority, if for no other reason than that I cut their hair every two weeks, an assignment I got because I said I could do it (I couldn't, but it was better than feeding the hogs).

The one older boy in the house, Arthur, was a tall, rangy, troubled kid who must have been about 15 and had been put in the Little Boys dorm because Big Boys was full. He had been a thorn for the old couple, but I didn't have much contact with him, save riding on the same school bus.

When I came down to get the boys moving toward their bunks, Arthur had a bunch of them around him watching TV and he refused to move.

I didn't want any trouble, but I intended to keep the house operating the way it was supposed to, thinking if it didn't, I might lose my spot, so I insisted, at which point, he attacked, flailing long arms and bony fists all over me. He was stronger than I could have imagined and as quick as a welterweight, punching, kicking and even biting when I grabbed him and pulled him close.

I was so startled by his aggressiveness that I didn't protect myself well and began bleeding at the lip and nose and hurting in several other spots. Finally, with blood flowing over my face and running down onto my T-shirt, making me look thoroughly banged up, I got him into a hammerlock on the floor. I didn't want to hurt him, but he was strong and his adrenaline was obviously pumping as he wiggled beneath me. "Arthur, dad-blame-it," I screamed, "get hold of yourself or I'll break your arm off!" At that moment, about five boys from the other dorm crashed through the front door and one of them said, "What's going on here?" They answered the call for help after one of the small kids—one I liked a lot—ran over to Big Boys to report the trouble and recruit some cavalry.

We ganged up on the Arthur, threatened him with death by commode flush if he didn't calm down and we got everybody to bed, a little later than I'd hoped. Arthur never gave me or the old couple much trouble again, at least overtly, though I never trusted what I saw. I heard he was thrown out about a year after I left for pushing some of the younger kids toward homosexual experimentation. Now *that* would have been a scandal.

*

There were some organized activities at The Home, but somehow I managed to skip most of them. I don't really remember how I did that, but I could be manipulative, even when I was happy.

There was a lake about 300 yards south of Little Boys dorm and a barn, where cows had been kept in years past, was maybe 300 yards north. The entire campus was large, open and as rural as I imagined anything could be.

The kids complained, as kids do, but life at Grandfather Home was good, idyllic compared to where these children had been—some abandoned, others abused, nearly all from homes where alcohol and drugs flowed freely. Food was plentiful, children who had been abused were nurtured and taught that they had alternatives, and they were clothed and educated by the church. Families within the Presbytery "adopted" children and sent them boxes of clothes and other necessary items at Christmas—the kids referred to them as their "packages"—and took care of other needs as they arose. The hospital treated the children free, as needed (hence my knee surgery and an open door policy on use of the whirlpool during sports seasons, which I took considerable advantage of). When a Grandfather Home child graduated high school, Lees-McRae would give him a junior college education free.

*

The town of Banner Elk, which was about the size of Cranberry, had a blinking yellow light on its main street, the only traffic light in Avery County, and a movie theater. We saw "Hercules Unchained" in that theater and that's about as good as the movies got—and about as recent, having been made in 1959.

Banner Elk sits at the foot of Beech Mountain, a ski resort these days, but when I lived at The Home, it was virgin territory. Beech was a favorite hiking place for a lot of us and we'd often hide in the bushes and watch the boys and girls from Lees-McRae, thinking they'd found some secret haven away from people, strip naked and wallow in each other. Our loud giggling sometimes gave us away and we'd get chased off by angry college students—naked as they were on their arrival dates.

The day it was announced that a ski resort was going up on Beech, some years later, an old friend called me and said, "I hope the hell a plane crashes into that big building they're planning and knocks it and everything else up there down. They ain't got no business building up there on that bald mountain. It's sacrilegious." I think my environmentalism, a defining part of me for years, began with the destruction of that beautiful virgin mountain.

*

Grandfather Home is still operating, but in recent years there was a scandal that had to do with abuse of one of the kids and the North Carolina Department of Social Services threatening its license. I don't know what happened and I don't much care. I can tell you, though, that when Miss Anne was there, there would have been no abuse, no scandal and no loss of license. This was an institution that was run the way it was set up to run and it gave kids—like me—a chance, a pretty good chance.

**Cranberry
High from the
football field.
The science
building is at
the right**

CRANBERRY HIGH

As much as I liked living at Grandfather Home, I genuinely loved the high school in Cranberry. I was made to feel at home the minute I got there. Maybe before that. Jerry Turbyfill—Turk, to everybody but me—and I had become friends over the summer and we were both newcomers. Jerry's family had moved up to Cranberry from Oak Hill, N.C., about 75 miles down the mountain, during the summer and we had football and girls in common. We were both awaiting football season and missing girls who weren't around. I had my first smoke—a foul-smelling cigar—on a trip back to his old home to visit his girlfriend.

Jerry and I had done some workouts together over the summer and about two weeks before school started, we showed up at the football stadium to try out for the team. Each of us did well at our respective positions—he a guard, I the single-wing equivalent of a quarterback—the first few days. When the day came for us to hit for the first time, everybody on that team wanted to know what we were made of and felt an obligation to try to kill us. I called Jerry the next morning and asked if he was as sore and bruised and cut and dispirited as I was and if he planned to go back. "Me, neither," I said, after hearing his painful grunt. "I've never been so beat up in my life and I've been playing football since I was about eight. I didn't know you could get hit as many ways as I got hit yesterday." Jerry grunted again. I took it as agreement.

We did show up, though, too stubborn, embarrassed and prideful not to. That afternoon, through our pain, gimpy joints and weariness, we extracted a measure of fierce revenge, leveling some of the team's best players in an effort to show that we could not only take a hard hit, but deliver one. We could hear the low "Ooooooh," when the pads cracked. The natives whispered and I looked over and saw the toughest guy in three counties—Carl Waycaster—grinning that big, toothy grin of his. Carl had knocked three years off my life the day before. During a two-on-one drill on this day, I hit Gaylord Andrews, a starting linebacker and all-conference candidate, as hard as I'd ever hit anybody in my life and Gaylord went down in a pile. "Shitgoddamntohell!" he blurted. A few minutes later, Jerry put down two players with one block. Late in the practice, we ran windsprints and I made certain to be in a group with speedy Jim Lafferty, the team's best receiver with almost legendary speed. I took off my clunky football shoes and I outran him. I heard some whistles. One of the veterans said Lafferty was drunk last night and that accounted for the result. Turk and I stayed around.

When the head coach handed me that green-and-white No. 27 game jersey a few days later, I felt like I'd earned it with blood.

*

After those late-summer practice sessions, a group of us often piled into a beat-up hunting car that smelled like whatever was in season and headed for Elk Falls, a four-mile trip down the Elk River, north of Cranberry and hard against the Tennessee line. That's where those of us who could dive leapt head-first off this huge rock, 15 feet into the icy water below. It didn't look like much, but I felt like an Acapulco cliff diver looking down on the flat, gleaming water, bending my knees, springing forward, slowly raising my hands over my head and entering the water with a lot more splash and thud than I intended. You could hear my pores slam shut when I hit the water and when we went in one after the other, some guys jumping, some all but falling, a farmer likely heard our screams a mile away.

This was life as I had only imagined it.

*

I wound up re-injuring my knee several times during the course of the football season (once when Jackie Buchanan, who found out I'd been talking to his girlfriend and that she liked me, hit me in practice with a cheap shot). I played little over the season. The only time Mom ventured up from Asheville via bus, and with Becky and Paul in tow to see me play, my knee was heavily taped, swollen and nearly inflexible. I played some, but she was disappointed. "I thought you'd be in more," she said, as we walked off the field following our only loss of the year.

"Mom," I pleaded, "I completed every pass I threw and had a couple of good runs. I'm playing with a bad knee."

"Well," she said, "you shouldn't play if you are hurt."

"You don't understand," I said. "How was your trip up?"

I performed passably well when I played, considering I only had one wheel (well enough to get the attention of an assistant coach at Western Carolina, who was scouting a running back from Mars Hill named Charles Tolley when we played). Jerry became a solid, dependable starting guard and led us to a one-loss season, that to Mars Hill High, the game Mom saw, costing us a conference championship.

This was backwoods ball and it was a hoot. We played on a sand field at Spruce Pine High; on a field with little grass, but plenty of rocks—which I threw into the stands—at Bakersville; and I was told that the field at Cloudland High over on the Tennessee side of the line through Elk Park was on the school roof. We played Cloudland at home, so I didn't get to see it. Crossnore came in with these unholy black-and-orange uniforms and Cane River had a 300-pound lineman. It was like running into the Pillsbury Doughboy. Turk's old school, Oak Hill, played at our place, 4,000 feet higher than their town, and after a half the players couldn't breathe. Jerry walked off the field in victory with his girlfriend, a dark-eyed, shapely godess from Oak Hill, the one he didn't marry and the one I liked a lot. (The Cranberry High girl he married, Doris, did well by old Jer, who wound up working in a glove factory in Spruce Pine. They had a bunch of kids and Jerry and the boys built a log cabin on Squirrel Creek.)

Carl Waycaster, a homeless, farm-working Cherokee Indian who "stayed" with people when he wasn't sleeping in barns or cars, and wrestled with a speech impediment, became a good friend. Carl was a defensive lineman on the football team and an occasional student who was probably mildly retarded. In all the years I've been involved with football in one way or another, I never saw anybody play the game as well or with as much abandon and pure joy as Carl Waycaster. He filled stadiums with both his hits and his wild laughter following every success.

I have this picture of Carl suspended in the air on a freezing and snowy November evening, stretched completely parallel to the ground as the East Yancey placekicker boots a ball into Carl's already-broken ribs. Carl screams in pain, then lets out this enormous war-hoop! He'd won the game by blocking an extra point and the ribs could wait until morning.

My mother—when we visited Asheville at Thanksgiving—was taken by Carl's curly-haired, square-jawed, gleaming white teeth good looks, cheery demeanor and excellent manners, but she couldn't resist picking at him over his speech impediment, which he thought was hilarious. They had a special connection I never figured out, but I guess it had something to do with Mom having a retarded kid of her own. Carl, like Jerry, turned out well; married, kids, good job, all of it.

*

The school year was a pleasant one for me. I liked the people and the work was easy. The school was so far removed from civilization that only about half the teachers had degrees. The school system didn't have any choice but to hire them because there wasn't anybody else. My two best teachers, Hop Heaton and Rock Hall, teaching geometry and English, had learned their disciplines in the Navy and junior college, respectively. The short, 35ish basketball and football coach, Buster Burleson (who had the school's only master's degree), had never lost more than one football game in a season and had never played a minute of any sport in his life. One of our optional classes at Cranberry was Mountain Dance and the school's square dance team was nationally known.

I'm not certain how much success the typical 1960s-era Cranberry High graduate could expect, but he could certainly expect to enjoy school even if it didn't prepare him for much later. Somebody once estimated that a Cranberry grad had an eighth-grade education and I thought that was being generous.

*

In late November of 1963, I had cut biology class in order to take a nap behind the football stadium before basketball practice. I regularly cut biology because it was taught by this hefty, 50ish space cadet named Elsie Bowers and she never suspected anything was amiss about anything. Elise was in a world not populated by the rest of us most of the time. When she called the roll, somebody answered for every name every day and she never noticed the perfection of attendance in her classes or who the voices belonged to. It wasn't necessary to go to class in order to pass it, because Elsie left her gradebook on her desk, opened with a pen lying across it, as if inviting students to put in their own grades, which some of us did. I cut her class six straight weeks at one stretch—including two while recovering from knee surgery—and finished with an A. I had flunked biology in 9th and 10th grades, and in summer school after 10th, but I didn't flunk it in 12th. It was a miracle.

Anyhow, I was lying on the hill behind the stadium—the "stadium" was steel frame and wood grandstands on one side of the football field (our barn of a basketball arena was called "The Coliseum")—half asleep when I heard this screech coming at me. "They've killed him; they've killed Kennedy," screamed Patsy Smith, my girlfriend, not my relative. I awoke suddenly, if not completely, and said, "Who killed who?"

"Kennedy, you dumb jock," she said. "They've killed President Kennedy." I was not especially impressed, political novice that I was and Kennedy fan that I was not. But I thought I'd probably better not say anything because I was seeing a passion in Patsy that I hadn't seen before and she was angry and hurt. I sat there for a while, listening to her and touching her hand occasionally as she cried. But I didn't feel much of anything.

That night, I watched Walter Cronkite review what had happened and what it meant. It was the second time in a brief period that I had been glued to the TV over a national event of huge importance. A month earlier, we had the Cuban Missile Crisis when Kennedy faced down the Soviet Union in Cuba and moved to the edge of World War III. Yet to come was the introduction of the Beatles to America (with Cronkite on CBS Evening News, Dec. 7, 1963, then in February of 1964 on the Ed Sullivan Show) and the British Invasion, which was not a military event. That floor model TV in the living room at Little Boys became a significant gathering place.

*

In the spring, when my fancy was supposed to turn toward getting into Patsy Smith's jeans—which I did not; I don't remember ever even kissing her (some girlfriend)—my knee started bothering me and the doctor over at the hospital told me I needed to have the cartilage removed.

The Doc (a nice guy who was to become a missionary in Africa) took cartilage out—both pieces in my right knee—and cost me the lead in the senior play, which I had, but gave up, since I'd be laid up for a while. I asked the doc to save me the cartilage and he said he would, but he later told me some girl had come by and picked it up, telling the doc I had told her she could. I never found out who in the hell wanted my used body parts.

*

I'd already been bounced from the basketball team for conduct unbecoming a Wildcat (Coach Burleson frowned on stealing jerseys from opponents' locker rooms, not learning plays and missing jump shots), so I was left with not much to do, except get in trouble, which is when my drinking began. It started one night when several of the boys picked me up in front of Little Boys and deposited me back there about four hours later a drunk and changed-for-life 17-year-old.

BECKY AND THE BABY

I wasn't surprised when Becky said she was pregnant. This was her fifth pregnancy. She was 19. I was annoyed, anxious and afraid of what we'd be facing. The previous four had been illegally aborted and I was pretty sure that's what she had in mind for this one. I hadn't been a part of anything that preceded this pregnancy and my only real involvement would be in its termination.

Becky and my friend Adam Salford, an enlisted airman stationed at Pope Air Force Base in Fayetteville, groped at a heated weekend romance for about six months early in 1969. Adam could only visit on weekends, but I was surprised how often he covered the 200 miles for a few hours of lust. He had hitch-hiked, flown in private planes, taken the bus, bummed rides from friends going west, and hopped an outbound tractor-trailer. He hadn't ridden the rails yet, but I guessed it to be only a matter of time.

Becky hung out at the cabin I lived in because home was difficult. Her dad drank heavily and her manic-depressive—bi-polar, these days— mother had unpredictable, radical swings in mood. Becky was given the run of the cabin and I liked having her around because she kept the place clean, she played with my kid, Jennie, who was about a year old, and she was nice to talk to. Jennie's mama, a beautiful German who married me to get out of a bad home situation, had left shortly after Jennie's birth. I had girlfriends who wondered who the hell Becky was and why she was at my place all the time, but I told them it was none of their business. Not many of them could get past that, but I guess by that time I had developed a certain loyalty to Becky.

She was a not-especially-pretty, dirty blonde, straight-haired, big girl with high hips and slate blue eyes too large for her small, triangular face. She had a thick waist, a large, round bottom on high hips, smallish, pointed breasts and narrow shoulders. Becky rose an imposing 5-feet-10, two inches taller than Adam and a shade taller than me, though she appeared to tower over both of us.

She was quiet most of the time, but when she was comfortable, as she was after a while, she could talk for hours. She was intelligent and sensitive, though she spent a good bit of time trying to hide that, especially when Adam was around.

She and I had had sex two or three times, but I felt guilty about it because she was Adam's girl. I don't think she thought much about it at all. Sex was simply trade to her. Make her feel good, you could have it. She'd been used so much in that way that I don't think she enjoyed it, regardless of who the guy was. She told me she'd never had an orgasm and didn't think she could.

Adam was often a heavy drinker who was loud and too attentive, especially to women, whom he'd paw to distraction. He was an information officer, peaceful duty in wartime. He wrote stories about visiting generals, base news items and awards ceremonies and I suspected that his duty frustrated him because he felt it beneath his capabilities. He had a square jaw, wide shoulders, small waist and he walked military erect. His hands were small and looked fragile, though the palms were calloused. His forehead was broad and his brow sloped forward, giving his eyes a dark, deep-set, brooding appearance. He rarely smiled, but when he did, he exposed small, even teeth, slightly off-white. There was that dimple that he hated for what it implied.

Adam was often angry and narrow, but he could also be tender and caring, as he played a sonata by Mozart on the piano, or clandestinely wrote a thoughtful short story or poem. He was often a contradiction, an enigma, a living oxymoron. Jung would have pointed to Adam when talking of the duality of man.

He'd been abandoned by his mother, betrayed by his father, and grew up in an institution. He was chaos.

Still, he was my friend in spite of and because of it all.

*

If I knew Adam would be in for the weekend, I wouldn't make a date and if he just showed up, as he did sometimes, I'd send the girl home and he, Becky and I hung out. I don't know why I preferred being a third wheel, but it worked out that way.

*

It was a nasty, bone-painful January day, claustrophobic and between the holidays and spring relief. Nerves flapped and Becky and I were in the cabin alone on a Saturday morning, with the day's first coffee and the paper. She looked at me for a long moment.

"I'm late," she said.

"For what?" I said, probably the only 22-year-old in Western North Carolina who didn't know instinctively what that meant.

"My period. I'm late."

"Oh. Very?"

"Nearly a month. I'm pretty sure."

"You mean pregnant?"

"Yes. Pregnant. God! I hate this. I hate those damn rubbers; they kill spontaneity, and the pill makes me sick and the diaphragm slips out. Besides, Adam won't wear a rubber, anyway. Says that's my job.

"I don't want to get another abortion, but I don't know what else to do. The abortion guy said last time that if I kept doing it, I might not be able to have kids when I'm ready. He said I could bleed to death easy. It hurt *so much*. I swear it must be as bad as having the baby."

She paused, crying, her face distorted as the tears cascaded off her chin onto her pajama top. I moved to the couch, sat beside her, put my arm around her. I didn't know what to say, so I didn't talk.

"If Daddy finds out, he'll kill me. I told him and mama about the first one and he beat me with his belt until I bled. Mama was screaming and he was cussing and I was crying. It was awful. Me and mama went to Charlotte and got it done. Daddy didn't know until after we got back and all he said was where'd I get the $100 and how I was going to pay it back? He said if I ever did it again..."

I squeezed her shoulder.

"That's when I stopped going home regular. At first, I'd stay away for a couple of days, then a week or so, then a month. Mama worried, but he didn't care, long as I wasn't there for him to have to spend money on. But he'd threaten me every time he'd see me."

"When will you know for sure?" I finally asked.

"I know. Really. This ain't new. But I'll wait 'til the end of next week and go to a doctor I know. We'll kill a rabbit and I'll set something up in Charlotte. Can you help me with the money until I can raise it and get it back to you?" There was a test at the time wherein a woman's fluid was injected into a rabbit and if the rabbit died, she was with child.

"Sure," I said. "I don't have it all, but Mike will have much as we need."

"I don't like him," she said. "He gives me the creeps. Can we get the money without him?"

"Becky, you know about beggars and choosers," I said. "We're not the choosers and there's worse people than Mike to deal with. He's always been good to Adam and me and we need to have an older guy on our side anyway, just in case anything went wrong."

"OK," she said, without conviction. "I just wish we didn't have to."

"Maybe we won't. Maybe this is a false alarm. You still believe in God, don't you?"

"Sort of," she said.

"Then pray."

*

Becky's gynecologist confirmed what she already knew and it was left to me to talk to Mike, to arrange some money and maybe even get him to drive us down in his 1965 Continental. I always liked that big burgundy ship. I remember the first time I saw it, I marveled at the leather seats, the sound system before there were sound systems, the sheer comfort. "What kind of gas mileage does this thing get?" I asked.

"What difference does that make?" he said. "Gas is 30 cents a gallon." It made a difference to me because I made $95 a week, which wasn't much even in 1969.

I'd first run into Mike at the Riverside lounge where he had brought in 25 newly-killed rabbits to be skinned and barbecued out back. He asked Adam and me to do it for a few dollars, free food and beer and we said, "Sure."

Mike was retired military and an insurance salesman who was successful.

Becky didn't know anything about Mike except that he leered at her. I expect he had probably kept his eyes too long on her breasts one day or maybe called her "honey" once too often.

"When do you want to go?" he answered my question without even broaching the illegality of the abortion, which wouldn't be legal for another four years, the expense, the time involved, the medical risks or the fact that Becky was a teenager who was all but a runaway. It would have been unlike Mike to respond any differently. I wished Becky could have understood that.

"Becky said the doctor has an opening early next Friday and I can still make work if we can get back into town by about 6:30 or so," I said. "I have to cover a basketball game that evening." This was a Thursday, so we had a day more than a week to get ready. I wished we could just go on down and get it done.

*

"Have you told Adam?" I asked Becky.

"Oh, God, no!" she said, louder than necessary.

"We gotta tell him. He's the father and he has a right to know."

"Why? The baby's in me, not him. I'm the one who'll either have to carry it or suffer through the abortion. He doesn't have to do anything. He just got his rocks inside me without thinking. It's mine and it's mine to get rid of."

"Calm down, Becky," I said, as evenly as I could. "How would you feel if the roles were reversed; if you had made him pregnant? Don't you think you would want him to tell you, to give you the opportunity to support him?"

"Dan, he's not going to support me, no matter what I do. He's just going to say, 'Well, you fucked up, didn't you? Take care of it.' That'll hurt me worse than just going ahead and having the thing and not telling him anything about it now or ever."

"If you don't tell him, I'm going to have to. He's my friend and he's your friend and he has a right to know that a baby he created is going to be aborted. He probably will act like an asshole, but at least we have to give him the chance."

I called him that night at the little apartment he had just off base and he was about half drunk. Becky was right about his response. He asked, "Whose is it?" That made me so mad I slammed the phone down.

He called me the next day at work, apologized, and asked if I'd get Becky to call him early that night. She called from the bedroom and they talked about 30 minutes. I finally went in and gave her the hurry-up sign because long distance calls were expensive and I didn't have much money. She was off in about three or four more minutes and came into the living room looking calm and relieved. "He was *so* nice," she said. "Thanks for making me call him."

*

The appointment in Charlotte was at the office of one Dr. Belding, a tall, dashingly-handsome African-American ("Black" in the vernacular of the time) physician who had all but openly set up an abortion clinic in the middle of the most segregated part of Charlotte. Belding closely resembled maverick Congressman Adam Clayton Powell of Harlem, who was later thrown out of Congress as a crook. He was known all over the state for his outspoken opposition to abortion laws—which he considered especially burdensome for poor people—and for his waiting room, famous for its privacy, its cheer and its expensive booze.

We didn't have any trouble finding the clinic because Mike knew Charlotte and everybody in town knew the clinic. It was in a plain, government-looking, one-story brick building with a glass front door and swinging saloon doors just inside—I swear to God—leading to the receptionist.

Dr. Belding met us out front and took us to a waiting room. "You must be the patient," he said extending his hand to Becky. "Yes, sir," she said, her head down. "Perk up, young lady," Belding said. "We'll have you fixed up in no time at all. You just go with the pretty nurse here and she'll get you ready."

He turned to me and stuck out his hand. "Mitchell Belding," he said. I smelled liquor on his breath. "Dan Smith," I said, "and this is Mike Heffner."

"Heard a lot about your waiting room," said Mike, laughing a bit too loud.

"Well, come right on in this way," said Belding. "We have several waiting rooms and I'll settle you into a good one." We walked down a hallway and stopped at a curtain. Belding pulled it back and we entered a plush lounge with stereo, television and full wet bar.

"You gentlemen help yourselves to whatever you want. I'll be back in a bit. I gotta clean me some chittlins." He grinned and walked out of the room.

*

The tall, slender, exotic nurse led Becky through a maze of rooms toward the back of the building, which was a great deal larger than it appeared from the outside.

The procedure room was brightly-lit, but the decor was functional and from the minimalist school: an examination/operating table with stirrups and knee supports in gleaming chrome in the center, a brushed chrome instrument stand with dilators, speculum, and curette neatly placed in a chrome pan, large cotton swabs, syringes and vials of penicillin, Demerol, Ergotrate and morphine. Becky was familiar with the tools and the procedures and detailed it to me later.

She undressed, hanging her clothes on a lone rack and slipped

Becky and my daughter, Jennie

into the green hospital gown, which stopped at mid-thigh, much like the mini-skirts she wore so often. She climbed onto the table, lay her head on the pillow and said, "How long?"

"Just a few minutes," the Jamaican nurse sang in her melodic accent, as she prepared the Demerol injection. "You'll feel drowsy directly." The nurse wet and lathered Becky's pubic area and shaved her in minutes. She swabbed the entire vaginal area with antiseptic, then left the room.

When Belding and the nurse re-entered the room together moments later, Becky was not yet totally under the influence of the Demerol, but the quiet conversation between the doctor and his assistant sounded miles away and the words were not clear. He looked closely at Becky, pulled her gown up around her waist and picked up the speculum, an instrument that looked liked it had two fingers, used to spread the vagina. He inserted it and locked it in place with a screw clamp. The Demerol kept Becky from feeling the pain.

Belding inserted the tenaculum forceps, which appeared to have dragon's teeth on the end, into the vagina and locked them onto the neck of the cervix, holding it still. He inserted the curette, a long steel stick with a scraper on the end, and scraped the wall of the uterus raw with it. The fetus was aborted in minutes.

Becky bled heavily after the curette scrapped an artery. Belding looked closely to be certain the uterus was not punctured. The light he wore on his head glared inside Becky and he detected no puncture, but he couldn't be certain. Had he had the time, had this been legal, he would have checked again in a couple of hours.

He packed the entire area with sanitary swabs to soak and retard the bleeding and gave her an injection of Ergotrate to constrict the blood vessels.

Belding burst into the waiting room with a smile that was as out of place as the wet bar. "Done," he said in triumph. Mike held his fourth bourbon and branch water, as he handed Belding an envelope with $100 inside.

"Let me give you a few instructions," said Belding, sliding the envelope into his lab coat. "Lay her down in the back seat of the car and let her rest all the way home. She may feel faint, short of breath, nauseous and she'll sweat a lot. Put her in bed when you get home and be sure she gets plenty of rest for the next three or four days. She'll lose a pretty good bit of blood and she'll be tired. Don't worry about the blood loss unless it becomes excessive and pools. Do you have a family doctor?"

"I think so," I said. "I'll find out."

"Is he somebody you can trust with this?"

"I think he's the one who told Becky about you." There was an irony in that: respectable doctors didn't perform illegal procedures, but they didn't hesitate to refer their patients, some of whom were wealthy. That is one of several reasons Belding was able to operate so openly. Nobody dared touch him because some of his clients were powerful.

"If anything at all happens," said Belding, "call her physician. He'll know what to do, especially if he referred her. Good to do business with you gentlemen. My nurse will bring your girl out in a few minutes."

He didn't even know Becky's name, I thought.

*

On the way home, Becky, who rarely complained, began to moan, softly at first, then more acutely as the miles passed. We stopped at a Texaco station near Hendersonville to check on her and found her dress and the back seat covered in blood. "We're getting her to a hospital," Mike said with a certain urgency.

We were all scared—both for Becky and for ourselves—when we walked into the St. Joseph's emergency room. We had a teenaged girl in serious difficulty and two guys who had literally driven her to it, illegally. Would Becky be OK? Would the doctor report an abortion? What would this cost, since Becky didn't have insurance? And, well, would Mike's leather interior be ruined forever?

We paced a stark, spare waiting room for two hours, and spoke occasionally. I bit my nails, Mike smoked constantly. A young man—not much older than me—finally entered the room and walked straight over to Mike. "You Becky's father?" he asked.

"Close as you'll get," Mike said.

"She's going to be fine. She was ruptured pretty badly during the abortion, but we got the bleeding stopped and she's young and healthy. It wasn't her first abortion, was it?"

"No," I said.

"Well, one of you is going to have to stress to her that abortion isn't birth control. It's also extremely dangerous, unregulated and damn-well illegal. No matter what I think, or what she thinks, or what you think about the need for it, that's the simple fact: it is not legal and you can do time for this. If it eases your mind any, I'm not going to report it because I'd consider that a breech of ethics. But please, please, please be careful."

I don't know that anybody was especially concerned at that moment about the potential for Becky to be barren, but it came up later. She'd played on the edge with her abortions, but didn't suffer long-term effects. She was married a couple of years after this incident and last I heard, she had five children and was happy. I was glad about that. She'd had enough of the other side.

I spent the Saturday after the abortion cleaning Mike's back seat and it shone when I finished—not a speck of residue—which pleased him. He quietly paid the $150 emergency room cost and when Becky found out, she smiled and said, "I think I might have been wrong about Mike."

**Coot, the last time I
saw him in the 1980s**

COOT

I'm told Coot's in jail to stay now, and I have no doubt he deserves to be there, but I wish he didn't have to be. Coot's the guy who taught me a lot about tolerating the intolerable, about laughing through fear and uncertainty, about staring down injustice, about being a good friend, about searching for similarities instead of dwelling on differences.

He was my first friend of a different race although our backgrounds included some of the same grinding poverty. He was the first Black person my age I had much of a conversation with, both of us about 19 and living hand-to-mouth in Asheville, on the make for a direction and purpose.

I'd rarely seen Black people as a kid in South Carolina. Racism was overt, institutional and devoid of embarrassment or apology. None of us escaped it, and once, as I awaited a bus to junior high, I heard a guy gruffly say "nigger" this and "nigger" that, as he railed with little purpose. I asked him what those people had done to him and he stared icily at me and said, "What? You some kind of got-damn nigger lover?" I was startled, humiliated and a little more world-wise because of that moment.

"Nigger" was a word that was used by everybody white, whether or not they meant ill by it. Mom and Dad said it the same way they'd say "German" or "Catholic" or "blue-eyed," as an adjective: "That little nigger-boy came by here looking for his mother yesterday." I don't remember any particular hatred or anger affiliated with their usage, though I'd heard other people say some pretty awful things about "Jigaboos," "Coons,"

"Bucks," and sundry other smears. They told how this race of inferior people didn't bathe, couldn't be trusted, were lazy, would steal anything not nailed down. A guy once told me to be careful about touching them, if I saw one, because the brown rubbed off. All of those references applied—at one time or another—to Italians, the Irish, Poles, Puerto Ricans and other minorities in the big northern cities, but it was the Southerners' particular stupidities that are best remembered.

The only Black people I'd see as a young kid with any regularity were part of a colony of Geechees, who lived across the Savannah River in Augusta, a city I've always thought of as America's armpit. These blue-black, short, sturdy women with big, black eyes, high cheekbones and hair tied with colorful scarves were a curiosity to me because they carried these large, round, heavy-laden baskets on their heads, and generally had one child by the hand and another locked on a breast. We rarely saw Black men.

I met Ernest—Coot to most everyone, save for his mother, a robust, woman with a big laugh who was to become a second mom for me—on a summer afternoon when the sun was direct and he'd just finished his work day at the Esso service station near the Kenilworth section of Asheville, where I lived. He was something of a mechanic trainee and he was stretched out on a stack of tires, his newsboy cap pulled down over his eyes.

Rob introduced to me to Coot and followed that with, "Aren't you getting a little warm there?"

"No, man," Coot said. "I'm getting a tan."

I looked at his skin, which was darker than a four-year-old football and grinned. "Y'all tan?" I asked, out of both ignorance and curiosity.

"'Course we tan," he said, pulling down his jeans to show a stomach a shade or so lighter than the rest of him. "How long you been off the watermellon truck? I thought you people was smart."

We both laughed and from that point a bond began to grow.

It grew through the James Brown concert in 1968 where mine was the only shiny white face in a crowd of about 3,000 people, some of whom wondered what the hell I was doing there, but most of whom didn't care. The ones who didn't like it took immediate note of the short, muscular guy next to me, a guy most of them knew at least by reputation, and decided that avoidance of fuss would be the wise course of action. Coot's girlfriend

Alberta tagged along. She was a pretty girl, short, ample, smiling, but as Coot stressed once, "They won't be naming no colleges after her." She later told me that several of her girlfriends asked after "that cute white boy," but she thought discretion the better part of valor, though she didn't phrase it just that way.

The bond between Coot and me evolved through double dates and ball games, lying in the sun and cruising Tunnel Road and out back at Buck's Restaurant where the drive-in was. It grew into a tight bond that we needed the day of the incident at Lake James.

Coot and Alberta, Gail and me and Rob and this redheaded cheerleader from Mars Hill College decided we'd go for a picnic and swim. We didn't think of the possibility that Coot and Alberta would not be welcome in McDowell County by the natives or their duly elected constabulary. Through dumb luck we managed to avoid a disaster, and escaped with bruised egos and a lesson in human interaction.

The good local citizens attacked almost from the moment we cleared the car and started our walk toward the beach at the lake. About nine young men in bathing suits—a couple of them sizeable and threatening—were shouting obscenities and it took a minute for Rob, the redhead, Gail and me to understand they were yelling at us. Coot and Alberta knew it from the moment they heard a raised voice. The men threw rocks and ran in short bursts toward us.

"We'd better get the hell out of here," I said, scared beyond anything I'd known before.

"Take off for the car," said Coot. "They want me and I think I'll let them have a little bit before I catch up with you."

"That's crazy," I almost screeched, pleading.

"G'won," he said. "I'll be right behind you."

Rob, Alberta, Gail and the redhead dived into the 1956 green Ford station wagon, the hunting car I'd bought from Al Geremonte for $100, as I looked back down the hill at that mob flailing at Coot. A couple of them were standing apart, holding their faces, blood pouring through their fingers, down onto one bare chest and one T-shirt. Momentarily another joined them; then another; and another. Coot looked up at us, saw we were safe, grinned broadly, hit one more guy square in the face, turned and sprinted toward us. I had started the car and threw open the door on the passenger side up front—the shotgun seat. He leaped in and we took off—in reverse because we couldn't go forward without plowing into the McDowell County warriors and it would have taken too much time to turn around. We backed up for nearly half a mile before I felt safe enough to stop and turn around.

In a few minutes we found a brown-shirted sheriff's deputy, who stood beside his cruiser at the entrance to the park. I began slowing down and Coot said, "Don't stop." But I did. I told the cop what had happened and he looked at me hard, his eyes vacant, his mouth turned down. He bent down and looked inside the car.

"Let me tell you boys something," he said as level serious as he could get. "We don't take to white people and niggers mixing here in McDowell County and we don't take to niggers swimming in our water. You'uns is lucky you didn't get killed back there and if you stay around here much longer or even think about coming back, that just might happen. Now you nigger-lovin' trash just git on out of here."

I don't remember ever before or after being as angry as I was at that moment. My face felt hot and my body shook with rage. I glared at that tall, thin, red-haired trooper with the Smoky the Bear hat, knowing that if I lost my temper we would all suffer a lot more than we had. Coot reached over and put his hand on my arm. I slammed the gearshift lever into drive and threw gravel behind us as we sped away. "Goddammit!" I screamed. "What kind of country is this? Who the hell are these people?" I pounded on the steering wheel, even as I floored the accelerator.

"Daniel," Coot said—he always called me Daniel when he was serious, same as my mom did. "That's the kind of shit we get every day. It's not always as out in the open as this. Those people hate us for no reason other than we're different and they're afraid. Me and Alberta knew something like this might happen, but we didn't say nothing because y'all were just so convinced we had to go swimming. I don't think it ever come to you that we can't do this without causing a whole lot of trouble."

"But why," I said. "Why? Why? Why?"

"Cause it's that way," Coot said. "Ain't nothin' we can do about it right now, so let's get home. Mama's got a pie waiting for us."

*

Coot and I ultimately drifted away from each other, as friends sometimes do. I moved to Roanoke and it was some years before I saw him again. He'd been a counselor in a juvenile detention center, among other things, but he'd taken to hard booze on a regular basis and he got into a lot of trouble. He had a quick temper born of seething, suppressed anger, and booze loosed the violence.

He said he was sent to prison for the first time on a manslaughter charge after he killed a huge railroad laborer with his hands in a bar fight in the early 1970s, while I raised a family and covered sports for a newspaper. During his jail time, his mother died in a fire at her house and Alberta married another guy. I got divorced again.

When I saw Coot next, he looked worn, was missing a front tooth and there was a sadness in his eyes, though his demeanor belied it for our short time together. He said he'd had it tough, but he'd learned a lot and he had quit drinking. I was happy to hear it. He deserved better, I said. But there was something basic absent in him and he knew I sensed it. He seemed embarrassed and that was new for us. We had been too close to being family for embarrassment to be part of it.

Coot didn't take to sobriety for long, and maybe he knew that was coming. Staying sober's hard to do for troubled people. There was too much inside Coot that hurt and booze medicated that pain. Rob later told me that Coot started drinking heavily again and was in and out of jails and treatment centers. Then he killed another guy the same way he killed the first one and they locked him up and threw away the key, Rob reluctantly told me .

I looked at Rob for a minute. "Damn," I said, and went off by myself for a while.

After the Times fired me in 1981, I discovered some
interesting career options, this one in Asheville

PART III:
WORKING

THE NEWSROOM

Anybody who has ever worked in a newsroom, especially a news*paper*room, understands why people who have been called "ink-stained wretches" generally considered other work beneath them.

The first time I walked into a newsroom—a late August afternoon in 1964—I couldn't see enough of it in my view shed. I turned around and looked at people and machines; listened to clattering, urgent noises; smelled cigarette smoke and coffee and paste and an asphalt- and oil-tinged breeze off the parking lot, as it wafted through open metal-framed windows. I wanted to touch something, and knew instinctively that a final level of stimulation would complete this sensual feast.

My first typewriter was a lovable old Underwood. I put racing stripes on it

As I sat in front of Bob Terrell's editor's chair in the sports department while he interviewed me for a "copy boy" job, my head continued to roam. His office had walls only rib high and above that I could see the activity at the city desk; I could watch reporters type and argue on telephones simultaneously; I saw the AP wire editor as he tore copy or watched AP photos as they rolled out of their machine in magical fashion, making a screeching noise. At one point, I heard Bob say, "Dan, are you listening?" and I realized I'd strayed from the interview. I said, "This looks like *so much fun*. I want to do it." I think the depth of sincerity of that innocent pronouncement from an 18-year-old who'd barely ever held a job got me a desk, a chair and a typewriter that I didn't know how to use, starting that day, that minute.

The pay was $5 a day no matter how many hours were in that work day, and Bob wanted me to work every day until I could type. Every day, no matter how many it took. He wanted me in the office at 4 and out at midnight. I was to type the whole time that I wasn't carrying somebody else's copy to the composing room—I was, after all, a copy boy—and he didn't care what I typed. As soon as I had a feel for the keyboard, regardless of how fast or accurately I typed, I would begin with briefs, then headlines, then captions. I would learn layout and be responsible for putting the paper out. All this before I could cover a game, conduct an interview, write a news or feature story.

Bob put the old warrior and outdoor editor Al Geremonte on me as my personal coach. Al, a Boston native and former platoon sergeant who'd fought at Guadalcanal, carried a blue editing pen and wore it out on me. He called me "Kid" in a thick Massachusetts-Italian accent and told me newspaper stories when he wasn't teaching me newspaper skills and I learned later that the stories are—in the long run—as valuable as writing, editing, layout and all the other things I had to learn to do. He gave me structure and purpose, a framework for a career.

Every day I came in, for the longest time, I passed through the door with the same wonder at being here, the sensual overload, the feeling that I was supposed to be in this place at this time, and that something good was in store for me.

It seemed only minutes before I could type well enough to get other assignments, slowly at first, then almost nightly for a while. I hadn't been at the Asheville Citizen for more than three months before I put out a paper by myself for the first time. I drew sports pages on layout dummies, read AP and local copy and corrected it, typed headlines, captions and all the rest, in a slow, careful, halting manner as I looked for the right keys. Al and Bob and Richard Morris and the one or two others who worked in the department up and left one night, saying, "It's yours. Do it right." And I did. Al had taught me how. I wasn't even nervous about it.

I was reminded about that night 20 years later when I was putting together a story on a 16-year-old skydiver and asked the boy about his first time out of a plane. "I was so well-prepared by the time I went out that I didn't think about it," he said. "It was easy." His main chute didn't open. "I just rolled over and popped the reserve," he smiled. "Didn't think anything could go wrong." And he didn't think anything *had* gone wrong? "Nope. That's why you have a reserve 'chute."

Al's the guy—with that one-on-one concentrated, selfless effort—who made me ready. He taught me writing with a simple, oft-repeated instruction: "Write the way you talk. Make sure you talk well. Be sure of what you're saying and be clear in how you say it. We're in the business of communicating ideas with clarity." Today teachers call Al's first instruction (write the way you talk) "voice." Al had an instinct for voice. When he wrote, I could hear the Boston in his upbringing and it wasn't just the accent.

He's the guy who stayed there day after day and pushed me, until one day he said, "You know, Kid, you're a pro now." I don't know when anything ever made me feel so good before or since. That night, over a beer at the Bavarian Cellar with Coot and a couple of other guys, I said, "Al called me a pro today."

"A pro what?" said Coot.

"Writer," I said. "*Writer.*"

Professional designations and "writes of passage" (Al's phrase) aside, however, the newsroom was its own reward. When I wasn't hunkered down editing copy—and wearing out an AP Stylebook and a book Al had given me, *The Elements of Style*—I was often in the wire room with an old guy named Deacon Smith. Deac laid out his thin cigars and cut them into thirds, then smoked one at a time, although I swear I don't remember seeing him light one. He'd been with Western Union 44 years, he said, "Quit. Didn't like it."

Deac was spending what should have been his retirement years ripping, reading and sending our copy out over the country from this tiny room at his little keyboard in front of one of those bulky AP machines.

I stood for a long while in front of one of the AP machines one early-morning and watched as it clattered: "Senator Kennedy Shot in Los Angeles," then read word by word as a story slowly appeared. I was so mesmerized that I didn't shout it out, just stayed right there and read it a word at a time, then heard the photo machine—with its tissue thickness of chemical-smelling paper—turn on and begin to rotate until I could see a black-and-white image form a line at a time. A man lay in a pool of blood, surrounded by others. The picture was close and filled with drama. I pulled out all the overnight paper from this long, narrow single sheet that fed the AP machine from a box, and went back to the middle-of-the-night "BULLETIN BULLETIN BULLETIN SEN. KENNEDY SHOT." I ripped it off and took it home.

*

I took part in the Vietnam War at those machines. "CAUTION. CAUTION. Dead body can be seen in Photo # 1432." "CAUTION. CAUTION. Offensive words on helmet of soldier in Photo #2364." A handwritten peace sign underscored with "FUCK WAR" was clear. "Impeach Johnson" on the side of a tank, a marijuana leaf on another helmet and a string of Vietcong ears around a soldier's neck drew advisories.

The night Jayne Mansfield was killed, I'd just finished the first edition and wandered over to the wire room where I saw a photo of a Cadillac as it was etched with the caption telling me, "Actress Jayne Mansfield died early this evening in a crash …" Later another "CAUTION" said her head was on the hood of the car where the support post for the roof would have been. I saw it, but you didn't, even if you got a newspaper. We didn't run those photos or the ones of her body lying in the foreground of a photo—car in the background—covered by a blanket, a dark, blood-soaked indention where her head should have been.

I stood at the photo machine shaking with laughter night after night as "streakers" ran naked through any event on earth that drew more than two souls, an attempt at some type of levity in a world gone totally mad.

*

I listened with fascination as Lewis Green, our best and toughest reporter, and Nat Osborne, our best and toughest editor—both of them combat veterans—screamed at each other, faces inches apart and bright red, over a city government corruption story Lewis had written and stood by, even though his evidence wasn't what Nat thought it ought to be. I listened a few weeks later when Lewis had his final argument with power—Executive Editor Dick Wynne this time—and stormed out to start The Native Stone, an alternative weekly that represented much more courage than substance.

I watched Al Geremonte, who had moved into the Sunday editor's slot after years as a sportswriter, take a 20-page Sunday cover story by Richard Morris on the Fellowship of Christian Athletes who were meeting at Montreat, and drop the last 15 pages in the can beside his desk. He said, "We'll start with this," then proceed to cut what was left to three pages. Richard, a short, red-faced, hot-tempered, slurring, ugly little 50-year-old gnomish bachelor who simply could not write a coherent sentence, was furious, shouting obscenities in the name of the Jesus organization. Al grinned and said, "You got any pictures with this?"

*

I watched as printers—Linotype operators, composing guys, plate-makers, pressmen—exited the locker room at work time, straight and tall, men with a purpose and with a skill going to work. They printed your paper, secured your freedom, like soldiers in the war both for and with the republic.

I stood amazed sometimes as reporters entered the newsroom at 11 p.m., fresh from a contentious City Council meeting, and yelled, "This one's good, better clear out a spot on Page 1," then sit down and generate steam from the old Underwood upright. Energy and adrenaline poured out into the smoky room as other reporters gathered around.

When I finally began to get out to events—mostly high school games of one flavor or another—I came in, like the others, excited, ready to write, and told my story to anyone who'd listen. "Man, you should see this kid who …" I'd begin to blank stares from veteran reporters, who saw me as an 18-year-old talking about 17-year-olds. It was what I had and, by God, I was going to tell it, then write it just like real reporters did.

During the few years of Civil Rights unrest and the 1968 presidential election with Richard Nixon vs. Hubert Humphrey vs. George Wallace, there were occasional stops by candidates. Race-baiting Wallace drew a big crowd to Pack Square in downtown Asheville where protesters and supporters got rowdy, and I watched from the sidelines with a real yen to get involved, but I knew I'd better not. The schools were finally being integrated, following a 14-year-old Supreme Court ruling, and there were daily rumors and reports of student violence, which threatened to spill over into the streets. There was constant tension, especially in the newsroom.

Sports became more relevant than usual, as black and white athletes began to mingle and test each other in an effort to determine if there really was a difference. I proposed a story from the athletes' perspective, but it was rejected for fear of "stirring things up even more." That resulted in my first battle for a story, which I lost. "These guys are at the front line," I pleaded. "They have to know each other, work together, get over any prejudices if they're going to be any good."

I knew the players, I said, knew the coaches, knew the students and the administration. I knew their parents and I wasn't all that much older than the football players. "They'll talk to me," I said. Doesn't matter. Can't do it. It'll cause trouble.

The rejection hurt and I was angry for days until Al took me aside and said, "You have to realize, kid, that there are influences at work here we don't understand. The potential for violence is very real and we have to be careful. We have a community to think about."

*

We were a smallish, 70,000-circulation, backwater daily newspaper sitting in the middle of a place where not much ever happened, but this was still a newspaper and it generated a kind of excitement in me that not much else—save football on a good day—ever had. I loved it here, loved the people, the work, the machinery, the smell, the noise, the confusion, the cigarette smoke, the arguments about ethics and courage, the fact that what I did mattered.

It has never left me, even during that dark period in the 1980s when I stewed at the bottom of the profession at a tiny weekly paper after my fall from grace, worked for people I didn't respect, grew bored with sports, found myself cutting corners and growing lazy, became an oft-married drunk, bad father and general lay-about.

But I had this profession when there didn't seem to be anything else and there were a lot of minutes when, as Paul Simon wrote, "I took some comfort there."

THE DRAFT

There were two basic fears among teenagers when I was one in the early- to mid-1960s: pregnancy and the draft.

Sexually-active girls, or those who were thinking about becoming so—and there weren't many of them, if my experience was a gauge—had a consuming fear of pregnancy, but not the draft, since they couldn't be drafted. Boys had to worry about pregnancy and the draft because each had direct bearing on our futures, especially with a nasty, under-publicized little war simmering just beneath the surface in Southeast Asia and the phrase "had to get married" not yet having found its way into quaint folklore. For my first 18 years, young men were subject to the military draft at 18. Not many escaped, even in peacetime.

On our 18th birthdays, boys were notified that we must register with the Selective Service, usually at some imposing government building in town, and at some point after that—it could be days, weeks or months—another notice of a pre-draft physical showed up in the mailbox. It was a notification most of us dreaded a lot more than a reminder for a dental appointment or the one telling us to show up in traffic court to explain those 14 unpaid parking tickets.

The Selective Service in Asheville gathered up draft-age boys occasionally and sent them to Charlotte on a bus to give them physicals at a military facility. The boys came from a pretty good-sized region around Asheville, a city of about 65,000 in the mountains of North Carolina and the largest city west of Charlotte. It was the hub of culture, finance, commerce and just about everything else for the rural mountains.

I got my registration and physical notices within a couple of weeks of each other just about the time I began working for the Asheville Citizen-Times in the sports department. I was holding two jobs and giving nearly everything I earned to Mom, to help with the meager Social Security check that came each month. The check was $179 a month. My total income was $50 a week, $40 of which went to Mom. She had to support four kids still at home on that.

By this time, I was out of high school a few months, back in Asheville from my year in Avery County where I finished school. I hadn't made many friends, and didn't have a car, so I didn't need money.

Fact was, though, that I fit the profile of the young man who would be snatched up by the draft board as quickly as I passed a physical exam because I wasn't in school, wasn't married with children, didn't have a big job in an important industry, didn't have a daddy who could pull strings, and I was poor. The military services have always loved guys like me.

But I had an ace in the hole and I was fully willing to play it.

*

I told my sports editor, Bob Terrell, that I was going to have to leave early Thursday morning to go to Charlotte for a pre-induction physical and that I didn't know if I would be back for work Friday night. He was excited for me. "A little time in the Army will be good for you," he said. Bob was one of those peace-time military service guys—post-Korea, pre-Vietnam—who thought every man ought to spend a little time under the boot-heel of a foul-mouthed, testosterone-soaked, sadistic drill sergeant because "it builds character and discipline." I knew—intuitively—better than to think that I would flourish in the repressive, brutal atmosphere he so outwardly cherished, as long as it wasn't him living it.

Bob was one of those spontaneous conservatives who always analyzed situations in the way that so many Southerners did: with simplistic jargon in order to avoid having to think about what was happening and come up with a considered solution. It was pure country intellectual laziness.

When—a few years after my physical—Muhammad Ali, whom Bob continued to call by his Christian name, Cassius Clay, announced to the world that "I don't have nothing against no Vietcongs" and that Ali, therefore, had no notion of fighting them, Bob immediately banned Ali's—and Clay's—name from the Citizen-Times sports pages. Take that, he must have thought. Without publicity in the Asheville Citizen-Times—MR. CLAY—your career will go straight to the shit hole. I chuckled inside when he banned Ali, but I didn't say anything. Bob could get pretty headstrong when challenged and I was still basically just a kid with no power.

When I told Al Geremonte, my journalism coach (we didn't have "mentors") and our outdoor writer, about the pre-induction physical, he grew serious. Al was an old warhorse platoon sergeant who had fought in some of the fiercest battles of World War II in the South Pacific. "Be careful what you say down there, Kid," he said. "You're not dealing with the intellectual elite here. Those military types will draft you on the spot if you say something they don't like, and you don't want to go into the Army right now. This Lyndon Johnson is going to have a lot of trouble in Vietnam [Al pronounced it 'Veet-nam'] because he's not smart enough to know how protective those people are of their sovereignty. Those Buddhist monks are setting themselves on fire over it, for Christ's sake. Just be careful and keep your mouth shut."

*

A group of about 50 white boys—the colored boys, I guessed, went on another bus—met in the lobby of the Arcade Building across the street from the Citizen-Times in the pre-dawn twilight that Thursday morning and watched as a man with military bearing, but in civilian disguise, barked instructions, lined everybody up, checked papers and generally organized everything before we got on the big chartered Trailways bus.

I was in line with a large, bushy-blond-haired guy from Spruce Pine—an hour north of Asheville—that I later discovered had played football against our team a year before on that sand-pit of a field that Harris High School called home. He had been one of the opposing tackles and I remembered his outline pretty well, since it had hovered over and chased after me for most of the night in a game we won as a team, but I lost as an individual, waking up the next morning feeling like somebody had shot me out of a cannon for a daring flight over the Toe River.

This big country boy—Joe Buchanan—had been primarily responsible for my post-game misery. In the huddle a couple of times, I pleaded with Jerry Turbyfill, a guard on the right side where Buchanan stood, to "please block that slobber-knocker before he rips my helmet off with my head in it." How prophetic. I can show you the front tooth my face mask chipped when Joe tore my hat off and the mask went into my mouth. Blood all over the place. The only thing I didn't like about football was its violence, especially when I was the violated.

Joe and I were placed in seats almost exactly in the middle of the bus, left-hand side, and I slipped around him in line and jumped for the window seat. "You coulda asked," he said.

"Wouldn't have been as much fun that way," I grinned.

On the hour and 15-minute ride to the induction station in Charlotte, Joe told me he worked in a mine just outside Spruce Pine on the road to Mount Mitchell and that gem mining was the major industry in Mitchell County. He said those mountains contained rubies, garnets, emeralds, topaz, rose quartz, sapphires, feldspar, and dozens of other precious and semi-precious stones—57 varieties in all. The feldspar and pure quartz were the primary focuses of the mining because they had practical uses that didn't include rings, bracelets or necklaces. Feldspar is used to make a variety of products from bathroom fixtures to Coke bottles. The quartz—almost all of the world's production is in Mitchell County—is used in electrical conductors.

Joe said his family had been in the mines since the turn of the century and he was a miner because he never thought about being anything else. He hadn't ventured any further from Spruce Pine than Asheville—this was his second trip to Asheville—and Charlotte would mark a new outward edge for him. Most of his travel had been on the football bus with Harris High School and that was for an hour or two on Friday nights.

Joe looked almost nervous as the bus pulled out, anticipating, I guessed, a new world out there. I asked him if he had any thoughts about whether he might want to join the Army and see the world and he said, "Naaaaaw, I'm just a miner. All I'll ever be."

We talked quietly as the bus made its way out of the mountains, through the hill country and into Charlotte, the biggest city most of the boys on the bus, including me, had ever seen. Charlotte wasn't then and isn't now big enough to make even a country boy wide-eyed, but it was a good bit bigger than we were used to and it got our attention.

The induction station was inside a fenced area in yellow block buildings, about as sterile as any buildings I'd ever seen. I can't fathom architecture schools training people to design these things. They had a distinct purpose, though, and that was to process American youth to see who was fit for slaughter. The military has always baffled me. Both my father and his brother, Earl, had experiences that could only be described as SNAFUs (that would be "Situation Normal, All Fucked Up") by even the most reverential militarist.

Dad, as I detail in another chapter ("Daddy Dies"), had decided after World War II ended that he wanted to remain in the Army as an officer, but it was discovered that he had diabetes and would need to be medically discharged (imagine General Motors dismissing a middle manager because he had diabetes). Dad was deeply crushed. He disappeared for a while— AWOL or Absent Without Leave, they call it. The Army found him, court-martialed him and sent him to federal prison for a year because he didn't say "May I?" before leaving, which is what the Army wanted him to do.

Uncle Earl, Dad's brother, had been deaf as a mole since rats damaged his ears when he was a baby, though he made it through basic training at the start of World War II without anybody making the discovery of his deafness. When the Army finally discovered that Earl couldn't hear the gun next to him at the rifle range, it gave him a medical discharge.

Earl lived on an Army pension for the rest of his life and Mom blamed that for what she called his "just pure sorriness. Earl's the laziest man God ever put on earth."

*

I've always thought that the selection process was thoroughly Army, which is to say a walking, talking contradiction. These Army guys examined us to determine if we were worthy of being killed. They wouldn't take us if we had bad teeth, wore glasses of a certain strength, didn't hear especially well or had weak joints. They didn't want homos, liberals, vegetarians, free-thinkers or perverts of any description. Just plain old crew-cut American youth, healthy of body, weak of mind. So we could get shot.

I looked about as white, healthy, crew-cut and ready to die for Democracy as anybody in line. But, as I said, I had a plan and that plan didn't include shootin' no Viet Congs or even trips to Germany or Korea to defend America. It had to do with staying in the newspaper business and becoming what Al Geremonte called a "pro."

All the guys, and there must have been 500 or so of us— a wild guess meaning "a whole lot of white guys"—were lined up against a dull-yellow tile wall and teams of what I thought might be Army doctors passed us, one after the other, checking various body parts and orifices. A dentist looked at our teeth and an eye doc gave us a test. One guy caused a stir when he said, "Bend over and spread 'em" and some of the guys didn't know exactly what he meant. You could tell which ones were the hayseeds because they were a step behind the rest in spreading 'em. Of course, everybody was reluctant to perform this delicate task, reminiscent, as it was, of what a homo might do in a public bath. But an order was an order and we knew we'd better do it.

Then there was this "psychological test" where, I think, they wanted to separate those with gender issues. I sat at a guy's desk, naked except for my underwear and listened as he asked if I was comfortable. "Sure," I said. "Why wouldn't I be?" The word "smartass" didn't fall from his lips, but it lurked close to the edge. The shrink wrote something down and asked questions about whether I liked my mom and dad, whether I'd ever been arrested or really mad at anybody and, he said, "Are you, or do you associate with homosexuals?" I don't think at that point I'd ever associated with a homosexual on purpose or even known quite what one was, so I said, "I don't know."

"Don't know what?" he said, his impatience growing.

"I don't know if I know. I never asked anybody. I'm not one, I don't think."

"Next!" he said, writing furiously.

I stepped back in line and the going-over continued, until this man in a white frock coat, open in front, stepped in front of me, looked me up and down and asked, "Do you know of any reason why you would be exempt from the draft?"

"I don't know, sir," I said, with my best military courtesy, "but I had my knee operated on last March and they took all the cartilage out of it. Doc Perkins said it would never be the same and that I couldn't play college football even if I could make the team." Doc Perkins had been right about the college football part, but the knee hadn't given me much trouble at all since the surgery, though the two scars were still bright red and I'd imagine every medical person in the building had seen them, since I wasn't trying to be subtle about their existence.

"You had any trouble with it?" he said.

"Well," I said, lying, "not a lot, but sometimes it locks up and I can't walk for about an hour. Doesn't hurt much, though."

He wrote something on the paper on his clipboard and said, "You can go get dressed."

I had just scored the biggest touchdown in my life and wanted to jump over the goal posts, but I got control and said, "Yes, sir. Thank you, sir." I wanted to salute, but didn't

*

A month later I got this window envelope in the mail with Selective Service written in the upper left-hand corner in official-looking government type. My stomach fell to my toes because I just knew it was a draft notice, despite my best efforts.

I reluctantly tore it open and read it carefully, especially under a section that told me I was rated "1-Y," which meant that I would be called several days later than a retired, one-armed, light-in-the-loafer, bomb building, Socialist Workers Party member from New Jersey. It was a classification given cripples and others of questionable function. I had been convincing and I was free—free in later years to even criticize the war effort that hadn't seriously started yet, if I wanted to (and I definitely wanted to).

At the Salem-Register in about 1988

NEWSPAPER STORIES

The stories started almost the first minute I entered a newsroom at the Asheville Citizen looking for a job as an 18-year-old who couldn't yet type, had no education, had never written a word for publication. 'Course I got the job. The sports copy boy had moved to the newsroom as a wire editor the day before and there was nobody left in sports to do the work. They were all columnists, famous guys who went to ball games, hunted, fished and golfed on company time, flew off in airplanes and smiled back at people who spoke to them in grocery store lines. Kansas City Star, that's what I are.

*

I guess it was Al Geremonte—who became the teacher to my apprentice—that got it started with his stories of the Notre Dame box formation; freshman football at Boston College where he saw the biggest people on the planet; shooting at a stubborn stag on Guadalcanal and watching as the stag stared him down in the middle of a dad-gum war. There was the story of Henry Logan scoring 12 points in 12 seconds and Western Carolina beating High Point by one; of Bob Satterwhite, who complained every day for a week about the "r" on his typewriter sticking, and coming in hung over one day, striking the "r" and calmly taking his typewriter to the window and where he dropped it into the parking lot. It became a kind of metallic sawdust. Bob was the guy I replaced. He became executive editor. He was quiet and didn't tell many stories. People told stories about him. Said he was crazy.

*

I told Al about my tryout at Western Carolina. I thought I'd play football for this new coach who was putting in a shotgun formation, close to what I'd run in high school. I was way too small and had undergone pretty serious reconstructive knee surgery in the spring of my last year at Cranberry High, but that didn't mean I couldn't play. I lasted a bit more than a week before one of the guys who was supposed to be there sent me home with a busted knee, a bruised ego and a broken heart. I thought I could do that thing, could make a mark with no special talent, save being able to throw a football well.

The day I left, I waited 'til the boys left the locker room to go out to practice and I went over to the big bin that held the clean jocks. I smeared analgesic balm—heat treatment for bruises—into the whole top layer of them. I'd have loved to have been there when they put them on, but they'd have killed me.

So anyhow, I'm back home, 18 years old, a college football failure, working in a barbecue joint—best dang barbecue I ever ate—for some Greek guys named Paulus, worried about whether my girlfriend is knocked up and having to see this storyline on my mother's soap opera about a young guy working in a burger joint worried about whether *his* girlfriend is knocked up. Every time I passed that TV show, I wondered if the thing actually saw into our living room. How else would it know? And so one day, I passed the TV and this voice says, "But you know I'm late ..." and Mom looks over and says, "You know, you ought to go by the newspaper and see if they'll take you on in the sports department. You've always liked to write and you seem to have a talent for it."

I never really thought much of Mom's ideas until that one, and I said I'd mull it over. Next day, Bob Terrell hired me and I never did see what happened with that guy who thought his girlfriend was knocked up, but Cynthia Foster turned out not to be. My luck was holding.

*

Bob Terrell, the sports editor who would go on to write a bunch of books, often told the story of these two guys from the composing room who'd go out to one of their cars every night and split a six-pack on their lunch hour. The beer sat on ice in the car. One night Bob brought a warm six-pack to the office where he, Al and I took turns shaking it. About five minutes to eight—lunch hour—he sneaked off to the car and replaced the cold beer with the shaken—not stirred—beer and ran back up to the second floor library where the whole sports department and some of the composing room guys lined the windows. The old boys got into the car and about 20 seconds later, both doors flew open and foam and bodies spilled out both sides, screaming and cussing and pointing to all those guys in the window laughing uproariously.

Terrell was an interesting guy, a mountain native and a man who loved to talk. He'd launch a tall tale at the slightest hint of interest ("I got the only picture of Billy Graham with a rifle," he once said, pulling the photo of the evangelist from Black Mountain, just outside Asheville, out of a drawer. "He loved to hunt, but wouldn't pose for a picture 'cause people might get the wrong idea") and Bob was a fountain of them. One of his favorites was the retelling of a story from his old buddy and Cincinnati Reds Manager Dave Bristol (1966-1969), who grew up in Andrews, N.C., down near Cherokee, where his father raised Russian wild boars.

These animals, brought into the mountains—where they had no natural enemies except us—at the turn of the 20th Century, were generally set free to roam the woods, make themselves at home and serve as game on occasion. Bristol's father raised these half-wild, dangerous animals on his farm and I remember a photo we ran in the late 1960s—shortly after Bristol became Reds manager—of him holding a pretty good sized hog up by its massive tusks. Bristol, his cheek bulging with a plug of tobacco, looked pretty tough to me in the photo, but his teams never broke .550 in a winning percentage and didn't finish above third in his 3 ½ years as Reds manager.

Terrell related Bristol's story of a buddy who'd not hunted these animals before, going out on a hunt and rousting out a big, nasty sow, who was not in a mood to be trifled with. The guy sighted in and cranked off a round, breaking off a big tusk and more thoroughly annoying Ms. Piggy, who snorted, scraped and charged to the horror of the hunter, who preferred to be at some kind of advantage and didn't seem to have one here. He slowly backed up, carefully aiming his rifle until he tripped over a small log and fell straight back. His gun landed between his legs, but was still in his control.

The hog continued to charge, 30 yards, 20 yards, coming hard. The man gripped the gun, aimed in a hurry and fired, hitting the hog between the eyes. She was about 10 yards away when the bullet struck and her front legs buckled, but her momentum carried her sliding across the ground until she stopped, one tusk in the hunter's butt.

*

Andy Wells was skinny Seminole Indian who covered stock car racing and often came back from Darlington or Daytona or some other exotic-to-me place with a car full of manufacturers' "samples," presented him with the assurance that he'd mention them in his column. He always did. It wasn't always pretty. He came in once with a car full of new tires and said, "Dang, I never thought I'd think about driving a station wagon, but it's coming to that. This stuff just ain't fittin' in that little car."

A couple of months later, he and I drove to Greenville, S.C., in his Shelby Mustang to pick up a brand new Dodge Satellite that he swore a company rep gave him. His next column was about Dodge race cars. About how they were the worst clunkers on the circuit.

To bring that Satellite home, Andy'd turned over the Shelby to me—a guy who drove a wrecked 1956 Ford station wagon that topped out coming off Beaucatcher Mountain at 38 mph—in Greenville and said, "Follow me and don't let me get too far ahead." Andy exited Greenville in reach of the sound barrier and by the time he hit Tryon, he'd was at warp speed. I roared out of town at 90 or so, scared half to death, and couldn't even find his tail lights.

The following Monday, Andy was stuck at the paper with no games, no races, nothing to do but watch me work and see what kind of stress he could cause in the newsroom. Andy loved putting darts into the vacuum tube that carried copy to the composing room, a lot like the one you put your money in at a drive-up bank. (My experience with the tube was to race a plastic copy carrying container that rode the tube back to the composing room. I won a good bit of money from people who simply could not believe I could outrun rushing air.)

On this day, Andy put in a dart and tried to outrun it on its path to the foreman's desk in the composing room. He and the dart arrived at just about the same second, an instant the foreman had chosen to put his hand on the end of the vacuum tube, something people did without thinking, like you put your hand into the wind out your car window. They got the bleeding stopped before the foreman had to go to the hospital and he got to say goodbye to Andy as Andy left the building for the last time, a former employee.

*

This guy was the same foreman who, in March of 1969, tried to have me fired because I spilled some type. Actually, spilled a lot of type. Eisenhower's obituary, it was. It'd sat there in type—which was engraved on lead slugs and put into forms, a line at a time, a mess waiting to happen at any given moment—for days while Ike hung on, heart attack after heart attack. He finally died and old Horace, our managing editor and a grouchy former Brooklyn Eagle reporter from the 1920s, had told me to go back and make sure the Ike pages were still there and were OK. He'd plug them into the paper and put a page number on the double-truck that would go in the middle of the paper as a special section.

The Ike obit was there. I rolled it from a corner in the back of the composing room toward the light so I could inspect it a little closer and dang if a wheel didn't buckle and Ike went flying all over the composing room. You never heard such cussing. From me and at me. That doesn't even count what Horace said when I said, "Horace, I dropped Ike," because he didn't actually say anything. He just looked at me. That was probably the uneasiest I've ever been and the foulest his mouth had ever been without opening.

They didn't let me in the composing room for months after that.

*

On a summer morning in 1967, a Piedmont 727 crashed after hitting a small Cessna in Hendersonville, about 19 miles from the office, and the police radios sounded like war. All our reporters, including me, were mobilized, ganged up into about four cars and headed to the site, where we saw the most awful scene most of us ever imagined—those of us who hadn't gone to war, anyway.

The smoke and the stink permeated every pore. There was a burnt-flesh smell I'd never known before, but identified without thought, perhaps by instinct. Pieces of people—and I don't know how else to say it—lay on the ground, on airplane fragments, on bushes, in trees. Whole arms and legs, torn off as if by a large wild animal, lay like pine cones in the forest. A man nearby was taking a gold watch off an arm wearing what was left of a white shirt and charcoal suit coat. I vomited as I got out of the back seat. I vomited again before I could look up.

I stepped over a small, disconnected hand and saw a whole head—a middle-aged woman's head with red hair, wide eyes, a horrified expression, her last. I vomited until I couldn't vomit any more; then I cried, on my knees, bent over to the ground.

After many immobile minutes, I went to work with the rest of the reporters, doing the only thing I knew how, since I had no training in this. I talked to people and put down what they told me. When I got back to the office, I wrote what they said and what I saw.

Nat Osborne, a quiet, deliberate, thoughtful veteran city editor on night side and a guy I respected, looked at it for a long time, his face pale and stark. He shook his head. He threw my pages into the trash can next to his desk. "We can't run that," he said, his voice shaky. I didn't even ask why. I knew. Nat went back to work. I went home. I was different.

*

Nat Osborne thought it would be novel to send a young kid sportswriter out to interview this old poet in Flat Rock on the occasion of the anniversary of some poem the poet wrote, see what I came up with. I never did figure out what the poem was—something about a road, I think—but it was a pretty day and a drive out into the mountains was almost enough to make me feel like one of the columnists: important and free, setting my own agenda.

Nat's instructions were spare, like always: talk to Mr. Sandburg about what he's up to; look around, get a feel for how he lives; *see what you come up with, Kid.* Nat always liked it when people saw what they could come up with. I didn't come up with much. What I found was a white-haired old man, pleasant enough, sitting on the porch of his fading frame house, a blanket in his lap, goats milling about. He had a fat, fidgeting, nice-as-could-be old housekeeper who offered me tea with mint. I told her three sugars and hold the mint.

I sat down and said, "Well, Mr. Sandburg, tell me what's going on."

"I'm sorry?" he said, puzzled.

"You know," I said, pretending to have some clue. "What have you been up to since you wrote the poem; what's important?"

It didn't get much better on my end for the next hour or so, but Mr. Sandburg didn't seem to have any place to go and he liked talking, so I listened. Don't remember much of what he said and, in fact, I didn't remember a whole heck of a lot of it when I got back to the office, either. I'd forgotten to take a note pad and pen, so I didn't have any notes. Or any idea what I'd just sat through. Nat just shook his head when I told him. "Kid," he said. "If you get any greener, somebody's going to pick you. Do you have any idea who you just spent half a day with?"

*

Several years later and 300 miles north, I was working one of those early-season Friday football nights in the Roanoke Times sports department. It was, I guess, the early to mid-1970s and Newton Spencer, Tony Stamus—they're both dead now—and I were the only people left after a furious night on the phone with coaches and managers calling in games from the boondocks. It was closing in on 11:10 or so and the TV was on in the background.

"Let's call Channel 10 and say the Salem Pirates' manager just resigned," I said. "Salem's out of town, so they won't be able to call the clubhouse to check."

The Salem Pirates were winding up their Class A Southern League baseball season with a series of road games. Newton and Tony howled. Newton dialed the number and Tony, who had a great radio-style voice, reported the scoop. Five minutes later it was on the air. It was never corrected or retracted. I always thought the TV sports editor at the time, a guy named Larry Draper, must have thought he dreamed it.

*

A little on into the fall, several of us were in the office late on a high school basketball Friday and the furious pace had dried up and we were bored again. "I know," I said. "Let's call the Asheville Citizen-Times with a basketball shutout. We can say Drexel beat North Carolina School for the Deaf. Both of them are on the fringe of circulation and they'll never check it. We can say the game is at NCSD. I don't guess you can call a deaf school to check stuff."

Newton reported the game, inventing—off the cuff—some of the most ridiculous names of basketball players I'd ever heard: S. Jumper, L. Shott, R.E. Bound, J. Bench, D.R. Ibble, B. Pass, L. Nett, M. Point, A. Guard. I.B. Tall. Tony and I were shaking with laughter behind Newton as he muffled the mouthpiece.

"It'll never run," Newton said. "There just ain't no way they're that stupid."

"Don't be so sure," I said, knowing those guys.

Our call was the lead sports story Sunday—we were too late to make Saturday's paper—my brother told me when I called Sunday to see how we'd done. The boys in Asheville had never double-checked.

*

By the late 1970s, sportswriting had become, in my mind, a cabin in the deep woods for intellectual deficients and had lost any appeal it ever had for me. It was a mind-numbing grind, night work, the same teams and personalities, the same conservative, anti-intellectual, dim bulbs day after eye-glazing day. I wanted out, so I made a move, begging my way into features, which felt like a soft, smelly, comfortable old chair to me.

Almost immediately I found people I liked, especially a long-haired, short, rimless-spectacled Santa Claus of a man, who reviewed movies, played bass in a rock band, talked of Southern gothic culture and literature. He had a mastery of language that often left me breathless. Chris Gladden had come into the news business the same way I did—through the back door—and was a better writer than most of those with specialized degrees and rooms full of awards. He understood the reader and he didn't patronize. He wrote with zeal, zest, humor and intelligence and he attributed when he needed to, not when the company lawyers told him to.

We started eating lunch together at 11:30—getting there before lines formed—just about every day and after some months of this, we had eaten at nearly every restaurant in the downtown district of Roanoke. It occurred to us one day that we probably knew as much about downtown food as anybody in town and maybe we should do a team restaurant review—or, more precisely a dueling restaurant review, given that our tastes were quite different.

Chris liked quality and I was in it for bulk. He'd grown up in a nicely comfortable family that appreciated finer things and I was one of eight children who, if they didn't eat fast, didn't eat. We went at it that way, he looking for the raised pinky, me the second helping. And, we wrote it that way, a dueling dialogue that read like a big-time magazine piece and stirred up the eat-out crowd. The story was wonderfully illustrated by a guy named Robert Lunsford, who did a stylized map in full color, which wasn't easy given the technology and printing capabilities of 1980.

The piece was good, but we found out after it ran that we didn't include all the downtown restaurants and the ones we'd missed demanded equal time. We had to go back and do a five or six-review follow-up for these hidden bistros—one a hotdog stand, for heaven's sake—and by this time our enthusiasm was drained. We'd been through the immediate elation of seeing the piece and the subsequent deflation of getting death threats—I got two from restaurateurs who didn't like what I had to say (and, oh, I was nasty to a couple of them who deserved it).

This story caused one additional problem: who got first by-line billing? I had seniority, but he had alphabetical supremacy on both his first and last names. We were generally considered to both be pretty good writers, so there was no break in that. We flipped a coin and he won.

*

The other deal here was that we had to determine if a shared by-line was a whole or a half, since it would figure into our weekly by-line war totals, tallied on Saturday. This had started months earlier when somebody noticed that each of us was out-producing everybody else in the features (cumulatively), news and sports. Each of us was setting standards of production that were ridiculous. We relished it, I think, because we loved what we were doing, we were good and it and we couldn't get enough attention.

(Let me also mention here that I was at a distinct disadvantage because I had to spend every Thursday—all of it—laying out our television section for the week and I didn't write a by-lined word on Thursdays.)

Our numbers started in single figures—about seven or eight by-lines a week each—but by the time our editor put the hammer down on the competition, we had finished a week with something close to a 24-23 score. I won a disputed victory when I wrote a piece that normally wasn't by-lined—the weekend "Tipoff"—in a way that gave me credit. The graphics people had begun running big letters with the start of each new paragraph in the "Tipoff" and spreading it across the bottom of the front of our features section. So I figured out a way to have the letters read BY DAN SMITH—starting consecutive paragraphs with those letters—and argued that was a by-line. The editor picked up that Saturday paper in the morning and I could hear her scream all the way across town: "Dan Smith, you devious son-of-a-bitch!" And blah-blah.

That ended the competition, but not the absurd production levels.

A few months later the editor fired me—and it's a long story having to do with my alcoholism, a love affair going into the toilet, difficulty with authority and anything else you want to throw at it, but I deserved it, even though the firing came on the heels of what Sandra Kelly called "the best employee review I've ever given anybody." Hey, you're only as good as your next story.

*

The disappointment in the firing wasn't so much being canned because I'd expected it, deserved it and was prepared for it. The hurt was that people I thought of as my friends, people I'd worked closely with for a couple of pretty intense years, people who'd been to my house, been fishing with me, heard my tales of woe and told me theirs, didn't even call to say they were sorry, to ask if there was anything they could do. Alone in that was feature writer Sally Harris, an old country girl from Galax with manners and a real feeling of responsibility for those around her. She'd probably been to scores of open-casket funerals. I always appreciated Sally for coming by.

I came to the conclusion that a firing is as close to a family death as we get at work without somebody dying. You're there, then you're gone, and people are bewildered, hurt and saying to themselves, "Thank God it wasn't me."

*

I wandered around for a while, gave away danged near everything I owned—including my Maxfield Parrish print, Johnny Rivers albums and Craftsman router—and headed for California and Mexico, trying to squeeze something out of myself that wasn't there at the time. I wound up back in Asheville for a while digging ditches with a guy who quoted the masters and picked his lunch every day from the flora and fauna wherever we were working.

I hooked up with a tiny newspaper in Vinton, a town just outside Roanoke, at the bottom of the journalistic food chain. I would be the editor said Don Smith, the publisher, dressed in bright yellow pants. He said I'd pretty much have the run of the place.

*

"Run of the place" meant I got to hire pretty young women as writers. It made for an interesting social life, though I suppose I should have come under some kind of investigation for it: "sexist, opportunistic pig," I think is the technical term. One of those lovelies was a funny, bright, mouthy, busty redhead named Patsy Jones, who worked for the gas company and desperately wanted to write. Thing was, she could. A natural. Didn't need much coaching and hardly any editing.

A couple of years later, after Patsy'd left her husband and gone through a series of jobs and men and moved to Charlottesville to live with her undertaker husband (whom she eventually left to go into real estate), I ran into her while she was visiting her mom in Roanoke. The talk turned to politics, which at that moment was dominated by the Clinton-Lewinski affair. "My oldest daughter came in the other day and asked me what I thought about Monica," Patsy said. "I told her I admired her, and my daughter's mouth dropped to the floor. 'What do you admire?' she yelled. 'Well,' I said, 'she had sex with the president of the free friggin' world. Best I ever did was a county commissioner.'"

*

Don Smith and his partner Paul Fitzgerald, a colorful drunk, creative, ambulance-chasing editor and a man who generated his own letters to the editor (according to his assistants), sold the Vinton paper and their other property, The Fincastle Herald, another weekly in the oldest county seat in Virginia (it covered territory from Virginia to Lake Michigan at one point) to Ray Robinson of Salem Publishing after I'd been at the Messenger for a few years.

Ray had owned the Salem Publishing products for a number of years and his background was that of a printer, which he did well. He owned a press that had been manufactured at the same time as those of the Messenger and Herald, but his always worked because he kept it in good condition, unlike Don Smith and Paul Fitzgerald, who tended to cut corners on maintenance.

I found Salem to be a lot like North Augusta, small, insular, snooty and closed to outsiders. It had a history of good sports teams, excellent schools and closed government, conducted in secret. Mayor Jim Taliaferro, to his credit, ran one of the most efficient meetings of any kind I'd ever seen, but decisions always seemed to have been made before city council met.

I never warmed to Ray, a round, bald, 50-ish, cigarette-puffing man, even though he eventually moved me to Salem as editor of his flagship newspaper and put me in charge of the New Castle Record, as well. Because good people had run through the system, and because the ST-R's small paper category has always been weak, the Salem Times-Register won a lot of press association awards. I won some of them, but was not pleased with my work there.

At one point, while Ray served as president-elect of the Virginia Press Association (later president), he won an award for column writing. His writing brought whispers of derision and rolled eyes from those who edited it. Ray was a printer, not a writer, so how he won the award always intrigued me. This is a man who once expressed to me this opinion of writers: "Type's cheap." I never entered the VPA contest again after his award.

Ray's wife handled the books, obsessed over the wedding page and stayed in a small front office. I had these visions of her stacking money, penny by penny, as she read the wedding accounts, anxiously looking for typos. She was not happy when she found one.

Ray personally delivered paychecks and once a year at Christmas, he'd hand out $5 bills in envelopes as Christmas bonuses. Our office manager in Vinton, Nita Echols, laughing robustly, once framed hers and hung it on the wall behind her desk.

(Nita, a proper Southern lady in her 50s at the time, was a funny bird. One day two very old women came in the office looking for directions to Oakey's Funeral Home. Nita drew it up and said, barely audibly but loud enough for me, "You might as well stay there." Another time, a woman came in complaining about her mailed newspaper delivery. After Nita explained that we weren't the Post Office, the woman looked at her for a long minute and huffed out. As the woman left, Nita said, "Don't let the door hit you in the ass.")

The Salem paper had (still has) one of the best small-town sports editors I ever knew, Brian Hoffman, a jovial, sweet-natured, generous, hail-fellow-well-met kind of guy that everybody calls "Hoop" and genuinely loves. He came down from Pennsylvania to Roanoke College, where he graduated in the 1970s, caught on with the paper and never left.

Hoop put in whatever hours were necessary to do his job, went anywhere, did anything to cover these Salem kids playing their sports and making sure their pictures got into the paper. He was, and remains, the paper's MVP, its real *raison d'etre*.

Brian once said, with a level of genuine gratitude, that Ray had given him some financial advice. Financial *advice*. Hoop appreciated small favors.

He fell in love with a pretty young composing room employee while I was at the ST-R. She was married at the time, and so Brian didn't let on about it and certainly didn't tell Doris of his feeling for her. But, occasionally, he'd stand up abruptly, stretch in an exaggerated manner and announce to me, "I'm going into the back to look at Doris for a few minutes." She finally left her husband, before knowing of Brian's feelings, and she and Brian have been happily married for years now.

At the Salem Times-Register, I didn't find the traits I admired in the classic weekly newspapers: courage, conviction, wisdom, grace under pressure, generosity of spirit, progressiveness, and a dogged insistence on doing the right thing even when the right thing is unpopular.

I finally reached a point where I couldn't work for Ray Robinson any longer and I'm sure he wasn't happy with an underachieving editor, either. I simply couldn't perform in a repressive atmosphere where Ray's mood determined the tilt of my day, so I went in one December morning and told him I wasn't doing this any more. He was neither surprised nor disappointed. It was be a mutually agreed parting. The bonus: it wouldn't cost him severance, unemployment or anything else inconvenient. I'd just go.

That night, Thurmond Andrew Horne, a guy I had known from AA during a brief stint there a few years before, called and asked if I could do a little freelance work for a new publication, the Blue Ridge Regional Business Journal, which was just about to publish its inaugural issue. I wasn't in a strong bargaining position and said, "Sure, I can. I can even be the editor if you need one." As it turned out, he did. He had fired his first editor, Tim Orwig, that day after one issue and I was getting ready to start the best job of my life.

*

Thurmond Andrew Horne was perfect as a follow to Ray. He, first of all, was a good guy, thoughtful, generous, intelligent, creative and eccentric. He was about 5-foot-7, bearded, thin and effusive. He bellowed when he laughed and made points in a loud voice that sounded like an exclamation point. He used his first name on occasion and his middle name on others. I always thought it odd that some people knew him as Andrew, others as Thurmond (that was for Strom Thurmond, the long-serving South Carolina senator from Thurmond Andrew's home state), but I never asked why he went from name to name.

Thurmond had been with Army intelligence during the Vietnam War and the word was that he had been significantly changed by the experience. His partner, Russ Hawkins—another guy I wasn't especially fond of—once told me that Thurmond lived with some tribesmen in Thailand and that they had something of a Joseph Conrad "Heart of Darkness" effect on him. Russ said Thurmond had been caught at customs, upon return to the U.S., with a seabag of marijuana. I don't know if any of that's true—probably isn't—but if there's even a grain of fact there, I would have no trouble believing it. I always hoped it was true, one of those "heroes of the generation" stories.

Thurmond did, indeed, fall victim to the ravages of addiction in a concrete way, though. He was caught embezzling money from Roanoke's Junior Achievement, of which he was director, and served some time in prison for it. That record, of course, made it difficult to get a bank loan when starting the Business Journal, but it helped explain his partnership with Russ, a man with whom Thurmond appeared to have nothing in common. Russ invested some startup money.

Thurmond hired me as a part-time editor at $300 a week (which is what I was making in Salem full time, but I could count on getting the check in Salem, not always the case with the Journal). All he wanted me to do, he said, was assign stories, edit them, write heads, do a little light layout and write a column if I wanted. If I did stories, I would be paid extra—he didn't add "when we have the money to pay you."

I don't remember exactly where I was coming up with money at the time, but it wasn't from the Journal and I don't remember minding that checks were delayed—once by 10 weeks. I understood that it was a struggle and that nobody else was getting paid, either. There was a camaraderie at the Journal that superseded money. We believed we were doing something important—me for the first time in years—and I, for one, wasn't going to carp on a detail that would either work itself out, or wouldn't.

Thurmond and I worked well together, though I could see where strong-willed Editor Tim Orwig and he might have clashed. Thurmond liked to have his ideas implemented and, though he would listen to good ideas and slide them in when appropriate, he had the final say. I suspect Tim resisted a bit too much.

I didn't resist at all because, although I knew journalism, I knew nothing about business or business journalism. I had a lot to learn and Thurmond had the vision. That relationship worked well for both of us because I got to learn and he got results from his ideas.

Eventually, Thurmond went as far as he could go with the journal before his past began to make a dent in profits. One PR shop owner smeared him every chance she got, which was often, and advertisers closed their doors.

Thurmond and I, returning from lunch one day, were walking directly toward this PR maven when he bellowed, "My god, woman, have you gained as much weight as it looks like or were you this fat all along?" She spun on her heel, huffed and stormed back the way she came.

This is the same woman who took one of her part-time employees—my old pal, Emily Brady (Carter), who was raising two kids by herself—to lunch on Emily's birthday, then deducted the price of the meal from Em's next paycheck. Class act, this one.

With the Journal in a corner, Thurmond sold the paper he invented and I was sorry to see him go. Always liked that guy. Still do.

*

Flash ahead a few years and as I drove my pickup truck back to Roanoke from Bedford, about 30 miles east, where I've had the Blue Ridge Regional Business Journal pasted down at the paper there. The technology's advanced to the point that we were dealing with all paper, all the time. I had to take the flats an hour the other side of Roanoke to get the Journal printed and time was tight. I had this pretty navy blue Toyota truck with a toolbox on the back that went out over the bed about 22, 24 inches and I'd slid the flats under it because moving air doesn't get down in there. I thought.

It was a gorgeous day and I was thumping along to Bob Seger's "Fire Lake," pounding the steering wheel to his piano when this flutter caught my eye. I looked around and it didn't repeat. Then it went up again. Still, I didn't see anything. I looked in the rearview mirror and watched in utter horror as the pages sailed out the back of the truck like so many white butterflies, lining U.S. 460 and making me the Litterbug of the Day, if not the Business Journal employee of the month.

**With the gorgeous German, Eva, my first
wife in 1967. We were 19 and 21**

PART IV:
LOVE NOTES

RINGS

At the Asheville Citizen, a little crippled guy named Maxey Guffey who operated a big, black, bulky, clattering-loud, smelly, hot Linotype machine, sold jewelry on the side, $5 down, $5 a week.

Maxey was an odd duck. He was a small man with a broad forehead, thinning hair slicked straight back, pointed chin and straight spine. He was forever cheerful as he dragged a useless right leg and a heavy brace and shoe behind him. Maxey'd suffered polio at some point, the guys told me, but he never talked about it, never made excuses for his handicap and would snap at anybody who tried to. He always wore a dark suit, white shirt and burgundy tie to work—looking more like a banker, or a jeweler, than a tradesman—where he'd make his jewelry rounds before heading off to the locker room and dressing in his olive coveralls for his day job.

Maxey sold jewelry for Finkelstein's and collected $5 per customer on his rounds. Often, you'd see people scrambling toward the bathroom, the locker room, the hallway as Maxey approached. They didn't have the $5 and had probably had already missed a payment. Maxey was stern with them without being harsh. "Jerome," he'd say, "you're going to need to come up with that money. I had the ring when you needed it and I need to get paid when it's due. When you don't pay, I have to."

Maxey got his hooks into me during a particularly vulnerable time when I couldn't figure out if I should get married or just keep trying—usually without success—to score without making what everybody kept assuring me would be a monumental, inescapable, life-wilting mistake.

Maxey always had a pocketful of wedding and engagement rings, diamonds, pearls, rubies, colored stones I couldn't identify in exotic colors and shapes set in silver and gold and platinum. $5 down, $5 a week and they'd be guaranteed to please any young girl, Maxey assured.

At 20 years old, I was horny all the time, but girls seemed to slip by me before I could get to third base. A couple of dates, a little slap and tickle, maybe a hand under a blouse or bra and I'd be left squeezing my pillow, frustrated and looking for answers.

Maxey offered up one answer with his rings. I don't suppose Maxey passed my desk without his hand out, palm up. He sold me a delicate solitaire diamond—probably ¼ of a carat ("It's bigger than it looks," Maxey assured)—for this girl named Gale Redmon that I'd been dating—a pretty, big-eyed blonde Arapaho with skin like silk on a baby's butt—who was making "serious" noises. I liked Gail an awful lot and we often sat in the front of my flake green 1956 Chevy—a hotrod that I couldn't drive worth a crap—and smooched for hours at a time, creeping close to heavy petting, but she wasn't going to let my hands or any other part of me creep below the belly button without some commitment beyond me saying, "But darlin', I love you. Don't that mean nothing?"

Gale was slow-moving, slow-talking and had those wonderful, blue bedroom eyes, a short neck and a shape that could only have been conjured by an artist. But she was no dummy, as a first impression would imply. Her IQ was off the charts and she was reading philosophy and physics, architecture and poetry for recreation. She and her father (her mother had left years earlier), who was vastly underemployed in some semi-menial job at the Veterans Administration Hospital just outside Asheville, talked politics far into the night. She was an innocent. I once asked her if she was having her period and she, stopped in mid thought, stared at me and said, "You know about *that!*" I know about a lot of things, I told her, overplaying a hand that wasn't much heftier than a couple of deuces.

I thought a ring would get me to the next step in our relationship without having to say anything binding, so I bought Gale one. She liked it and said, "Does this mean we're engaged?" and I said, "Sure." She liked that and went straight and told her father, who was less than euphoric. "That boy's just not much good," he warned, "but I won't stand in your way if you think it's alright." He likes me, I thought.

Several weeks later, Gale threw the ring at me late one evening, standing on her front porch after a night of me groping her in fruitless frustration and me finally proclaiming, "Gale, I just don't think this is going to work out." I spent the rest of the night in her yard on my hands and knees grumbling and trying to find the unseeable, her father watching over me, repeating to nobody in particular, "I told you he wasn't no good. Told you."

Maxey told me when I asked that, no, the price of the ring didn't include insurance for loss during a lover's quarrel and that I'd have to eat the loss and keep making those $5 payments. "That's hard, Max," I said. "You know I don't make $50 a week."

"Well," said Maxey, "you need to think about these things ahead of time. Investing is a serious bidness whether you're investing in the stock market, an engagement ring or a woman. Gotta think it out."

Maxey the philosopher, the jeweler, the cripple who won't act like it, the financier, the Linotype operator at the end of the era of this magnificent machine, one that was almost perfect for scores of years.

The Linotype was invented in 1886 by watchmakers—a small coincidence for Maxey—and to the day it became obsolete (there are still a few in operation as this is written in late 2006), it was still made by watchmakers because of its intricacies. Thomas Edison once called it "the Eighth Wonder of the World."

The machine came along about 400 years after Johann Gutenberg invented moveable type, allowing the printed word to be set a letter at a time. That method was still used when I was a young news-guy, but only for headlines larger than 24 points (about half an inch). No, I don't know why. Never asked. Those guys in composing were like mechanics or computer techies: they had proprietary information and if they were asked a question, they'd give a heavy sigh and launch upon an impossibly complex answer, demonstrating their vast superiority in their narrow area. It was galling.

A veteran operator like Maxey could produce about seven lines of type a minute. Each of Maxey's keystrokes on a regular-looking, but bigger, keyboard in front of the 7-foot-tall, 6-foot-wide and 6-foot deep monstrosity dropped a letter at a time from a magazine until a line—line-o-type—was finished and adjusted for fit; the machine then assembled a row of molds (matrices, they were called) with the character imprints. Hot lead was poured—by the machine—into the molds, forming a line, which dropped one at a time into a vertical stack at the front of the machine.

When he had a full stack, Maxey would put it into a long, narrow flat metal container that looked like half a cookie sheet and when the story was completely set, he would roll ink and then paper over it, making a proof to be sent to the newsroom (via my pal and colleague Andy Wells' favorite vehicle, the vacuum tube), along with the original copy, a series of the reporter's written pages of paper pasted together by the editor, in longer stories. Every reporter's desk had a pastepot, a small metal container with a screw-on lid and a brush attached to the lid. Frequently, you'd hear somebody bellow, "Goddammit!" and you knew he'd knocked over his pastepot.

(AP copy was set automatically by its own Linotype machine. The AP operator, upon the editor's request for a specific story, took what looked like ticker tape from the AP machine to the composing room, where he inserted the yellow tape into the Linotype, flipped a switch and, like a player piano, it cranked out its lead tune.)

Maxey's own type was eventually put into page molds, the makeup man using a hand-drawn page layout from the newsroom telling the composer what went where. When the page was finished, if I hadn't spilled it by then, it went to plate-making where another thick, pink, paper-like mold was imprinted by rolling a heavy piece of metal over the paper and lead was poured into the new mold, creating a metal plate for the printing press. I never knew why the paper mold was pink, but I often wondered. Didn't fit with the macho image of all those guys working with hot metal and growling at me for being alive.

Maxey loved setting type and I guess that's why he never gave it up for the potentially more lucrative and much cleaner life in jewelry.

THE MARRYING KIND

The question that ultimately follows my admission of having some ex-wives is "how many?" and I almost never give a straight answer.

Generally, I'll say something like, "Well, depends on what you count hahahahahaha. You know I was a drinker and drinkers forget hahahahahaha. Of course, there was a hot night in Tijuana that I don't usually count, but I guess I could if I knew the details hahahahaha."

"No, really."

And I'll finally have to say—with borderline rudeness—"I ain't tellin'."

And I ain't, usually, because multiple marriages—serial monogamy—sounds tacky and insincere and flaky and irresponsible and just stupid.

That's four marriages, if you don't count Kathryn twice, which I do sometimes because it's true, but almost nobody understands without a detailed explanation which I don't want to get into.

The numbers are impressive when you think about it: four (or five) marriages, five ceremonies, four women, two kids with different mothers, three divorces, three mothers-in-law (one orphan), any number of ex-relatives and all the remorse, guilt, conflict, romance, comedy and repercussion implied and realized.

Nita Echols, who managed the office of the Vinton paper when I was editor, once yelled at me, "Your ex-wife's on the phone."

"Could you be a little more specific?" I said.

*

The weddings were as different as the brides.

The first wedding, in February of 1967, was in an Asheville church office, presided over by a Baptist minister and neither Eva nor I was a Baptist. But we weren't anything else, either, except painfully young: she 19, I 20.

The setting made as much sense as anything else and, mostly, it fit a very small budget. The cost of the minister was $5 and I think I probably bought Eva a flower of some kind for a buck or two. The license came in at about $3, so we pulled off a sawbuck wedding and got what we paid for.

The marriage was over just about the same time we discovered the bride was with child, which was almost immediately. I married Chris a few days before the State of North Carolina declared my non-union with Eva history. Eva had taken off and left me with the new kid, but I didn't have a bad feeling for her over it. She'd had a tough time, being adopted and raised by people who didn't like her, and was sensible enough to understand the mommy gene missed her.

The Chris wedding was a bit more elaborate than the Evafest, set at Craggy Gardens on the Blue Ridge Parkway with family and friends in attendance, me in a tux, Chris in a wedding gown. All very normal, except that as I muttered, "I do," I knew I didn't.

Chris and I divorced after nine years and I thought, "You know, maybe I ought to cut back on this marriage business," and held out until the early 1980s when Kathryn and I got married twice in a week: once in Virginia to make it legal, the second time in North Carolina so family and friends could be there and we could go on a whitewater rafting trip that Kathryn dreaded.

She fell out of the raft, nearly drowned. I did my best hero to the rescue deal to pull her out of the icy, rushing water and onto shore. She slapped me. "I told you I didn't want to do this," she yelled, as the people in the raft at the center of the river cheered, not hearing the conversation. "You never listen." She walked back to base camp and I went back by raft.

The marriage lasted about five weeks. It was dead solid over when she had a nasty wreck on the West Virginia Turnpike on her way to visit her mama. She realized while lying in her hospital bed what an awful mistake she'd made.

For the next 20 years, all the weddings in my life belonged to somebody else and the demand was so pent up that when Christina and I finally wed, we had a rip-snorter, the kind of wedding a man can love. We did up the clothes, the catering ($4 apiece for a slice of cucumber topped with a mysterious paste) and the details. We rented the Hollins University Chapel for the wedding and the elegant Green Room for the reception. Sheila Trunzo, my pal from Lynchburg, baked a towering, gorgeous Italian wedding cake. Friends and family entertained: Betsy Gehman, a former big band singer, belting out "Skylark," Evan and his fiancé Kara signing and strumming "If I Were a Carpenter," my pal Steve Hartman, a former professional horn player, doing "My Funny Valentine" on the flute, poet Judy Tynan reading a special verse and missed-his-calling-as-a-standup-comic Rod Carter giving the "hominy" ("Love Is Like a Peanut Better Sandwich").

Christina's mother, obsessive about decorum, was mortified that Evan and I were in tuxedos at 11 a.m., so to mollify her, we wore bright orange socks and I hitched my pants so she could see them as I walked down the aisle.

This one, I thought, ought to take.

Christina and me: 'This one, I thought, ought to take'

My Favorite Ex-Wife

It always gets a laugh. "Yeah," I say, "my favorite ex-wife, who was 5-foot-2, broke my nose with this thunderous left hook and I'm laying back on the chair I landed in, bleeding and laughing…" or, "There was the time my favorite ex-wife and I were riding through New Mexico for the first time, climbing this great vista at sunset looking out over a painted valley and I say, 'Man, isn't this beautiful?' and she says, 'I wonder what it's like in Arizona right this minute?' Or when I tell the story about growing up and I say, 'I was telling my favorite ex-wife that the people I grew up with in the mountains of Western North Carolina were poor and not well-educated, but they were happy, and she looks at me and says, 'Oh, they just didn't know any better.'"

*

They want to know more about this ex-wife, but I won't tell them.

I don't talk about the intense green eyes, the flowing, lavish dark-chocolate hair, the snow-blind white teeth, the freckles sprinkled across her nose like paprika, the laugh that takes her over, shakes her, leaves her limp. I don't talk about the intelligence, the wit, the intense curiosity, the creativity, and a passion the likes of which I'd never even imagined. I don't mention that she was left-handed and ever-so-slightly pigeon-toed, that her stomach was board flat and her shoulders a pinch too broad, that she had small, alert, perfect breasts. It's all become my secret, the place I don't much want to go both because there is so much there and because there is so little.

While we were together those five years—I was 33, she 26 when it started—the world became a different place, full of colors I'd never seen, and one of those colors was a deeper black than I knew. But the reds, the yellows, the oranges, lit it up like airplane landing lights, like crystal drugs only imagined. We were a movie, a poem, a dance. Sometimes the movie was "Love Story," often "Psycho." The poem was alternately "Annabelle Lee" and "Evangeline," the dance a waltz or a wild-eyed flamenco.

There was rarely a middle to anything between us. We sat on edges and loved and fought and pushed and pulled. It was too much and it burned itself out like a flare in the rain.

We met in my living room. I was standing in front of a new-lit fire as she was pulled through the front door by Nancy Adair, our mutual friend and a woman with whom she worked at a child care center. Nancy was doing the "have I got a girl for you?" tour and the minute I saw Kathryn, dressed in overalls and a long-sleeved, horizontal-striped polo shirt, bra-less, a bow in her hair, I was smitten. That first night after Nancy left, we read *The Mason Williams Reading Matter* to each other twice, she reading a poem, I a chapter, she going again. We laughed so much it became painful and I think that if at about 4 a.m. we had both died, we would have been content with that.

I suspect people in general don't have many nights of such unbridled happiness as we shared that night. I know I haven't. One, maybe two others, but none shines like this one and I don't exactly know why, except that it was followed by days, months of such intense feeling, a consuming longing that bordered on psychosis.

The backside of that joy was its equal, wearing black, much of it the result of my intensifying alcoholism.

*

I had first been married at 21 in an immature fit of lust. My wife, Eva Maria Senne—named for Hitler's wife Eva Braun—told me she was the daughter of a Nazi tank commander and a German hooker. She'd been adopted by American Air Force parents in the early 1950s. Eva—and her brother, whom the Air Force couple also adopted—became their domestics, Eva told me. I say, "she told me" because I have no way of knowing if she was telling the truth and telling the truth was never a personal attribute, like her distracting natural beauty. She was tall, shapely and intense, with deep brown eyes, an oval face with perfect complexion, long dark glossy hair with an ancient Egyptian neck and an air of a young wounded animal.

When I met her, she was in business school and I was taking a typing class there. I had recently started working at the Asheville Citizen in the sports department and hadn't yet learned to type.

It was grab at first site, marry at second. She was as physically striking as any woman I have ever seen. A classic beauty, but temperamental and brooding. We had no money and no prospects, but plenty of interest in the game at hand and so we got married on a slow week and she got pregnant instantly, like snapping fingers: presto-change-o. What was doomed from the start was then double-doomed with a baby on the way, one neither of us anticipated or welcomed.

*

Eva stayed around for two months after Jennie was born, then was gone. Not so much as a, "Fare thee well." She wound up having an affair with a guy I thought was my friend. Best friend, he said.

Before the divorce was even final—by about two days—I was married again, this time to Chris, who agreed she'd make a good mother for Jennie. I never loved Chris and never especially liked her, but we stayed married for nine years, through thin and thinner, almost enough to cure me of the urge to do it again. This marriage got off to an ignominious beginning: I spent our wedding night in jail, having gotten drunk after the ceremony. I insisted on driving and asking a cop for directions with a 16-ounce Miller High Life between my knees. The cop was not amused by my stupidity or my verbal abuse as he hauled me off, handcuffed in the back of his cruiser. Let me amplify the bromide that there is no dignity in the back of a police cruiser.

Chris and I had Evan a few years into the marriage, the single good result, and one that she gerrymandered, she later admitted. I spent those years with her alternating between heavy drinking and trying to quit. I did neither well.

We divorced when I pushed the issue by getting involved with a pretty young blonde, married neighbor—not one of my shining moments. I was dumped by the kid (and I think I'll hang on to her name) pretty quickly after she saw what we were getting involved in and I look back on my part in the affair as more a desperation move than a relationship. It ended a marriage I had no idea how to end. I was free again and not at all unhappy about it.

*

Then Kathryn showed up and the aimless life I had known took on a cloying, frenetic character that I think we both saw immediately as destructive, but had no power to dodge. We were sliding down a pine-needle hill, waxed paper on our butts and a precipice awaiting that we saw, but didn't fear. Our physical and emotional pace would not be stemmed. I drank to get a perspective, to sharpen the already-brilliant colors while dulling the dread of this thing's imminent collapse. Kathryn looked for satisfaction outside. I brooded, she cheated and the circle began to spin until we were both flung from it, me losing my job, my family, my home, she taking off for Minnesota and another lover.

In the early days of the five-year on-again-off-again, world-of-our-own creation, there was a lot of gauzy highlight film: canoe trips down the James River, live theater and Kathryn's first ballet, hiking along the ridge of the Carvins Cove compound then skinny-dipping in the lake, picnics on the Blue Ridge Parkway, concerts and festivals and baseball games, art openings, comedy clubs and parties, lying naked in the rain in a Floyd County cow pasture, nights in front of the fire, her head on my lap, a favorite TV night with "Hill Street Blues" and "WKRP in Cincinnati." I rushed home for lunch and for dinner eager to spend even a few minutes with her after stumbling into the office late in the morning because I didn't want to leave her. She met me at the door each time with an eagerness that astonished me.

I'd never known anything like this intensity, this full-flower endorphin rush 24 hours a day. I didn't think it would ever end, but knew my body and my mind couldn't keep up with it indefinitely.

My drinking intensified, though I didn't notice at the time. She did and she mentioned it. "You know," she said, "I am involved with two different people and I only love one of them, the sober one. I don't like the other one."

She got pregnant and had an abortion without telling me until afterward. I was hurt by what that said. I had no idea she was pregnant until she showed up late on a Wednesday, having disappeared for more than a day. I was frantic with worry. She had never done that before.

"Where were you?" I said, more confrontationally than I meant. "I was out of my mind. I even called the cops. They're looking for you."

"I had to take care of something," she said, so matter-of-factly that it further agitated me.

"Kathryn, do you think you could tell me what it was? Don't you think maybe you should have said something before you left? Didn't you think I'd worry? Didn't you think I'd care? Didn't ..."

"Whoa, whoa, whoa!" she said. "Slow down. It's not a big deal. I wasn't out screwing around. It wasn't something that concerned you. It was just something I had to take care of and it's done."

"Would you please just tell me what it was, Kathryn. It's not like we're casual acquaintances. We live together; we share our lives. You are important to me, obviously more important than you know."

Kathryn and I married after living together nearly five years, off and on, but the marriage only lasted about five weeks

"I was pregnant, if you have to know, and I got rid of it. Simple. Done. No sweat."

I sucked in air and sat down.

"You had an *abortion*? I didn't even know you were pregnant. Kathryn, for God's sake, you could have told me; I would have been there for you. Jesus."

I sat, looking at the floor.

"What could you have done?" she said. "Nothing. Absolutely nothing. It was my pregnancy, my baby, my decision. I just did it and now you don't have to worry about it."

"But it was mine, too," I pleaded. "I shared in making it. We could have at least talked about it. I would have supported whatever you wanted to do, but do you think it was fair to leave me out of it, just go do it and leave me worried to death about where you were?"

"Dan, listen. This is not going anywhere. I was pregnant and now I'm not. End of story. Let's just drop it." She turned and walked into the bedroom. I sat there, tears running down my face, realizing what was happening, but not knowing what to do about it.

*

She tried during this period to tell me how she was feeling about us, but I didn't listen. She didn't complain often and never loudly, but she was in pain when I drank and she began calling a friend in Minnesota, a guy who cared for her and whom she was beginning to depend on for support.

Finally, one day after a night of tearfully watching me slowly destroy myself, she said, "Dan, I can't do this any more. I love you, but I have to take care of myself and you're destroying both you and me. I'm going to Minnesota."

And she did. Just about the time I was fired from The Times. It all fell in at once.

I think that by this time, the kids were numb to anything that was happening to me. Jennie certainly was. Evan may have been a bit too young to know or care.

I hit the road for California, giving away everything I owned that didn't fit in my truck. It was a self-imposed exile, a planned escape to nowhere. Empty adventure over the hill.

My trip and her trip lasted nearly a year. I spent some time in San Diego, then moved to Asheville and worked as a laborer before being offered the job in Vinton, a small Roanoke suburb. I moved back up to Roanoke and Kathryn wasn't far behind, joining me and marrying me, a desperation move that lasted a little more than five weeks. We went whitewater rafting on our honeymoon and she fell into a relatively small Class II rapid, giving me the opportunity to rescue her. As nice as that sounds, I don't think she ever forgave me for exposing her to danger.

The marriage was a disaster from the day we made it legal. We were married in Roanoke, then again three days later in Asheville for reasons that don't matter much, but two times nothing is still nothing.

Kathryn determined after about three weeks that she would visit her mother in Kansas and three hours after she left, her mom called and said Kathryn was in the hospital in Charleston, W.Va., having fallen asleep at the wheel on that god-awful, never completed West Virginia Turnpike (it was near noon, but she was emotionally and physically exhausted). "She's pretty banged up," said Mrs. Rhoads, who, for good reason, never liked me. "I hope you can get over there." It didn't occur to me for days that officials didn't call me; they called Kathryn's mother.

I was working day and night on the 100-page Centennial Edition of the Vinton Messenger at the time, but each day for more than a week at about 3 p.m. I left work and drove the five hours to Charleston, sat with Kathryn until about 10 and drove back. I didn't drink during that period. But it was too late.

When she got home, she had a distant look in her face, as if she had awakened from a horrible dream. She left almost immediately and for the next empty, exhausting 15 years, her ghost hung over everything I did, everything I felt, everything I couldn't be. I couldn't succeed, couldn't completely fail, couldn't love, couldn't feel. I had involvements, but they stayed emotionally at arm's length with no chance of getting closer.

For years, a fragility followed me, one I hid by being emotionally unavailable, distant. Intimacy, once such a strong force within me, was gone. It was difficult to look a lover in the eyes, to say something tender, to be romantic at any level other than with gifts. They were easy and they didn't commit.

I once told a woman I couldn't quite care enough about—though I should have—that the sword of Damocles she saw above my head was named Kathryn. The woman shook her head, slammed the door and left. She already knew.

PART V:
HAVE A DRINK ON ME

Slouching Toward Oblivion

It started that January night in 1964 when a couple of my high school football teammates, Jerry Turbyfill and Gaylord Andrews, and George, son of the shop teacher at the high school, picked me up at Grandfather Home. We set out in George's 1959 VW bug, which is why he was along, to "get some beer." I wasn't quite sure what that meant, but I'd been pretty well cooped up in my attic room at the children's home for a month and getting out under any circumstance was excuse enough.

"Getting some beer" in Avery County wasn't easy, even for those with money. Avery was dry and that meant we had to go to a bootlegger. Gaylord's next-door neighbor—in Avery County that equaled half a mile—sold booze out of his house, an open secret, which is pretty common in dry counties, since sheriff's department employees drink, too. The drive to "wet" Watauga County was about 30 miles on curvy roads, nearly a two-hour round trip.

The thin, pale, bald and most often pleasant bootlegger and his hefty, snarling wife lived halfway up a steep hill in a small board-and-batten house that seemed to be sitting there awaiting a puff of air from a passing butterfly to knock it off. A few years after I'd graduated from Cranberry High and left Avery County to return to Asheville, Jerry told me the bootlegger's wife attacked the bootlegger with a kitchen knife, stabbed him 11 times and that two months later, after he'd left the hospital cobbled back together, they'd reconciled. Patient man, he was.

Gaylord returned to the car with a six-pack of the worst-tasting beer I was ever to drink in my entire storied career—Falstaff—and two pints of liquor, bootlegger special brands called King Kong and Cobb's Creek. Even at bootleggers' prices and even in 1964, the whole package hovered at less than $9.

My first reaction to the Cobb's Creek was to bark, "Oh, Jeeeeee-zus H. Christ, Godalmighty!!" and I was the one who never swore (which changed the minute booze passed my lips for the first time). I was drunk before the bottle made it around to me again and I knew intuitively that booze and me were headed for a long relationship—and, I suspected, judging from what I saw of my father's alcoholism, probably not a good one.

An hour later my initial suspicion was supported as I made my way around the Ruby's Diner parking lot on my hands and knees, slurring, "I think I got fl-rosis of the liver" and I vomited, a dry Ralphing Buick, since I'd neither eaten dinner, nor drunk enough to dampen a towlette. But, boy, did it wallop me. It felt good, took me somewhere I'd never been, gave me space and peace, and the next morning my first hangover. Oh. God. It was awful. But unfortunately, I got over it.

*

The first DUI came on the night of my second wedding. I spent that night in the Transylvania County, N.C., jail, having asked a cop for directions, a beer resting between my knees as I sat in the car and he leaned in. He obviously smelled my breath long before he saw the beer and my first bust was set in motion. I'd wind up with three official DUIs in all and about nine more stops when I should have been busted, but laws were more lenient and cops tended not to want the hassle of the paperwork.

It was the second DUI, this one about two years later and in Roanoke, that introduced me to AA. A visionary judge named Jim Brice gave me the option of a series of AA meetings or jail time and you can only imagine my initial burst of enthusiasm for AA. That was when I picked up my first white chip, the poker chip you get when you tell everybody in the room that you've had enough and that you want to get better. "The only requirement is the desire to stop drinking," the man said. Well, I sure had the desire to stop, at that moment.

In AA, the guys giving out white chips often say it is the most important chip. I've never thought that. It is the easiest one to get. All you need is to be sick and depressed and miserable and to show up at an AA meeting, whether or not at the court's direction. It's the one-year chip that I found to be satisfying, maybe because it took me 23 years to get it. It's been on my key chain for years.

Booze—beer mostly because I never developed a taste for liquor or wine, nor an interest in drugs—led me into and out of two marriages by the time I was 30. (When somebody says "Oh, I can't be an alcoholic; I only drink beer," put on your bullshit protector suit. Alcohol is alcohol and alcoholics are allergic to it.) I had two kids by then but nothing to note in the way of accomplishment, save a few journalism awards that were mostly meaningless (I won a sportswriting "lifetime achievement award" *when I was 26*, the Marshall Johnson Award). I was singing the old John Conley song straight into my Miller High Life:

I'm on the back side of 30 and back on my own
An empty apartment don't feel like a home
The back side of 30, the short side of time
Back on the bottom, with no will to climb.

I'd made a stab or two at getting sober, but I never quite understood how AA worked and it was far easier just to go get drunk and forget it. Out there by myself, losing jobs, running across the country looking for God knows what, digging ditches, working for small, bad weeklies; none of it was working.

It was about 1985 that I made what looked like a stab at sobriety that would take.

Kathryn and I had split, reconciled, split, married, divorced and I was hovering around the edges of hope that we'd try it one more time when on my birthday, July 31, she was supposed to come over and I found out about 8 o'clock at night that she'd gone to the beach with a new boyfriend. I was crushed, but not drunk enough to be suicidal (for years, I awoke daily wanting to be dead).

I sat there on the bed of this small apartment in the down-and-out Belmont section of Roanoke feeling sorry for myself, trying to cry, having no tears.

Being in Belmont would have been enough to push most people over the edge. I called it "Fort Apache" because the most dangerous thing I did every day was go from my door to my truck, exposing myself to possible thuggery. I was working at the bottom of my profession at a 1,200-circulation newspaper in a Roanoke suburb, living in a house sitting among homes listed as "derelict" by the city planning department with a neighbor who'd once tried—in a pointless drunken rage—to break through my front door with a Samurai sword. I'd been robbed at least three times—there may have been more, but drunks don't often notice unless what's stolen is the size of a canoe, one of the items they got from me. I had the kids every other weekend in this dump and both they and I were embarrassed and uncomfortable with it. I think their mother was, too, but she needed the break and didn't complain about my living situation.

Here I was sitting in despair on the side of my bed and it occurred to me to call AA. I hadn't been in the program for some time, but I knew how it worked—at least on the surface—and I even had these "sober dreams" about AAs coming to get me, looking like characters from "The Night of the Living Dead." Alcoholics getting sober commonly have "drunk dreams," but I swear I never heard of a drunk having sober dreams, especially when the bad guys were the good guys.

I dialed the number in the phone book, talked to the guy who asked if I'd been drinking and I said what all drunks say, "I've had one or two beers." He said he'd send somebody over to talk to me "shortly."

In about 15 minutes two guys named Tom showed up at the door and I was immediately put at ease by them. One, the late, great Tom Shirley, a department head at Virginia Western Community College, would become my sponsor. The other Tom, a TV executive, was smart, accomplished and a good talker. I don't always like men because I find so few with interests that are beyond the narrow, but these were my kind of guy: smart, funny, genuinely masculine, self-assured, accomplished in a real sense, personally courageous and not afraid to feel something.

I was back in the program quickly and actually took a shot at working the steps and following directions, something that had escaped my attention in previous ventures. As my sponsor, Tom directed well, giving me at least the slim chance I'd never had before and he accompanied me to meetings, talked to me over lunch or on the phone, advised and pointed me toward activities that were good for me, none of which included old friends (who were mostly gone anyway), old haunts, old habits. I was feeling pretty good about everything—I still have some writings from that period and they are generally upbeat—but it fell apart again about nine months in and I wouldn't see AA again for nearly a decade.

Years later, after I'd returned to the fold, I asked Tom why he thought I had relapsed. "Because you're an alcoholic," he said. "Drunks drink. It is unnatural for us not to drink. You'll fight this uphill for the rest of your life and it never gets easy or safe. But I guarantee that if you stick with it, you get better in every sense."

*

I landed a job in 1989 with a brand new publication, The Blue Ridge Regional Business Journal (Regional was later dropped). In its second month of publication its editor had left just about the time I got fed up with a terrible little editing job on a small-time paper in Salem, the Times-Register. (I'm sounding pretty big for my britches when I talk about these little weeklies, but they were bad. And, frankly, they were right for me at the time because I wasn't a bit better than they were.)

Thurmond Andrew Horne, who owned the Journal, was a recovering alcoholic, who knew I drank, but hired me anyway. He was gone a year or so later and new ownership, Jim Lindsey, was in place. I was still drinking daily and heavily, looking for something I simply couldn't find, hoping to find something to fill the hole in the middle of me. The booze didn't do it, nor did anything else.

*

For about five years, I was involved with a woman, Suzan Bright, who had a couple of little girls that I cared about, an unusual distinction for me at that point. I could have killed them on any day. I drove them to ball practice and to a variety of other activities, drinking beer out of a 32-ounce lidded foam cup through a straw so the cops wouldn't know I was drinking and driving.

Everything I did, I did with that 32-ounce cup full of beer. My life, in general, was not that much different from other people's, except that the alcohol created a version of Cicero's Sword of Damocles, hanging by a horsehair over my head wherever I went. Always, there was the possibility that in an instant any tranquility I knew would turn to horror, whether because of drunk-driving, alcohol-induced mood changes or something as simple as losing my small paycheck, which Suzan called my "allowance."

Example: Julia, Suzan's oldest daughter, is probably the best natural athlete I've ever seen, but she was a sweet girl who didn't have a competitive nature. She was on a softball team, playing a variety of positions well, but had never tried pitching. In about her fourth game—I had driven her there, beer cup with straw in hand—the team's pitcher didn't show up and the coach asked if she'd do it. "Yes," she said, always compliant, "but I've never pitched before."

"No problem," I inserted briskly. "I'll teach you. "We have 15 or 20 minutes." Oh, here was my chance to save the day, to accomplish something. I took her over behind the stands with a softball, showed her the basic fast pitch motion, moved 45 feet away and said, "Put 'er right here, kid." She did. Thwack! The ball came with astonishing speed and accuracy, nearly knocking me on my butt from my catcher's crouch—a position I hadn't been in since I was about 12. "Oh, my!" I bellowed, grinning. "I think we have ourselves a pitcher." She popped in about 20 more straight, searing strikes and I made the profound pronouncement, "You're ready."

My goodness, was she ever. She struck out the first three batters she faced on nine pitches. The kids were big-eyed and disbelieving. This small, thin, pleasant little girl was throwing like Nolan Ryan.

At the inning break, she came over to me, sat down, dropped her glove and stooped her shoulders in something that looked like disconsolation. "I don't like pitching," she said.

"Julia!" I said. "What do you mean?" I took a long draw on the straw in my beer.

"I don't like embarrassing those girls. They're my friends."

A few innings later after she'd decided to let some of the opponents' players hit the ball—one out, one hit she figured was fair—there was a play at the plate following a slow roller to the shortstop. The ball was thrown to Julia instead of the catcher—don't ask—and she chased the runner toward the plate, reaching out at the last minute to make the tag." "You're out," the umpire shouted, thumb in the air.

Julia turned and looked at the ump. "I didn't touch her," Julia said. "She was safe." The umpire didn't know what to do. Nobody'd ever argued that she'd missed a call in that way before.

But that was Julia, a thoroughly admirable human being at 10, my hero already. (She went to work for the CIA after college.)

I watched Julia, held a beer and looking through half-bleary eyes, knowing I'd have to drive her home in this state, and knowing I didn't know how to stop doing what I was doing. The scenario would have been scary if I'd been sober enough to feel anything.

*

It was at Julia's mom's house that the habits that were slowly killing me began to change. My relationship with Suzan was nearing its end and I was looking around for changes to make. We'd had a pretty good run, a relatively comfortable relationship—if not one full of passion or devotion—and I didn't want it to end. So I thought I'd quit smoking. That would be a positive move. I had puffed away, 3 ½ packs a day for years, following a family tradition.

Dad and Mom smoked, he Chesterfields, she a foul menthol cigarette called Kools ("because that was all I could get during the war and I just got used to them"). The last thing I heard at night before Dad started snoring—another Smith family trait—was his smoker's cough. It was the first thing I heard in the morning, a death-rattle coming from deep within him and racking his entire body for minutes. I had it later and it always gave me a throbbing headache.

Julia and her sister were constantly on me about smoking. It bothered them, made them nauseated and smelly, and they didn't like it one bit. At work, I had to smoke outside. I couldn't visit certain people's houses because of the cigarettes. I was becoming even more a pariah than alcoholism had made me. So, at midnight, Jan. 31, 1993, I puffed my last.

It was a "sick and tired of being sick and tired" moment and I knew this would be the last cigarette. Putting down cigarettes was the first piece of evidence that just about anything can be overcome when it's time to do it. The body—my body, anyway—simply said, "Enough!" and the broken grip of addiction followed logically, a short, but not wholly uncomfortable, step at a time.

A week or so after my last cigarette, I bought some of those "quit-smoking patches," but after the initial withdrawal phase, I didn't need them (insurance, inexplicably, didn't pay for them, either). For once, changing a habit was relatively easy and it was the most difficult habit of all to change. Cigarettes (more precisely, nicotine), I read, are more addictive than cocaine.

A year later, when the time came to stop drinking, the process was pretty much the same. I just stopped. AA, like the patch, was helpful, but I think I would have toughed out the withdrawal without it. AA was far more useful later when I didn't know what to do with myself, didn't know how to live "normally," because I never had.

DRIVING DRUNK: A LOVE STORY

I suppose if I hadn't gotten sober when I did, these days I'd be resting fitfully and semi-permanently in a six-by-nine, mist-green, cinderblock room with indirect lighting and no toilet seat.

That's what you get when you drive drunk in the modern world. In other times, the cops were as likely to say, "Well, son, you g'won home now and don't let yo' mama know you been a-drankin'" as they were to bark, "Boy! You busted; bend over and spread 'em!"

I heard that admonition far more often and far later in life than I had any right to hear it. Nine times was I pulled over for "suspicion" and even at that, I was getting stopped about one in 1,000 times I could have been. Twice I was actually cuffed, read my rights, and pushed—hand on my head so I wouldn't bump it on the car roof—into the back seat of a police cruiser. There's no dignity in the back of a cruiser, especially when you're in Transylvania County, N.C., on your wedding night and the cop is just really pissed at your stupidity and arrogance "Jeeze, you Nazi!" I yelled. "I just got married!" This was during the 1960s when all cops were Fascist pigs, and all arrests were political to those of us who had any inkling of anti-Vietnam War sentiment.

The policeman who busted me, Frank was his name, sprayed mace in my face (that smarts!) and slammed the cell door so hard it nearly broke off its cinderblock moorings. "Eat vomit, you little snot!" he yelled back with less Southern civility than I might have expected from a man of his stature.

Drunk driving was one of my great pleasures for many years. During a lengthy sobriety, I've learned that I am not alone in my warm fondness—shrinks call it "euphoric recall"—for those moments of bliss in the evening sun, wind on my face, buzz in my head, the Animals yowling "I gotta get out of this place!" on the radio, Blue Ridge Parkway vista to the side, rollover lurking in the next curve. A common refrain in AA meetings is, "God, do I miss driving when I've had a couple of six-packs. I think out of everything I had to give up—and that's everything I had: marriage, home, kids, job, bank account—I miss drunk driving the most."

Career drunks, a distinct social class, surround ourselves with the like-minded during our practicing days ("practice" used here the way a physician would use it, not the way a football player would). The favorite of all my drinking buddies was old roomie Doug Smith, who was not related to me, but at times could have been me.

Doug had a habit of calling me from jail late at night. Once, early on a Sunday morning, I groggily answered the phone—I'd been drinking, but made it home safely—and heard, "Can you come get me?" "Ooooh, man," I whined. "Where are you this time?" Madison County, he told me, and the jailer was the meanest sumbitch he'd ever offended. Chased him around the cell with mace for 30 minutes before letting him call me.

Madison County is north of Asheville, by about 30 miles and 100 years. The people there during the time we're discussing were old mountaineers, poor, uneducated, backward in every sense. They were clannish, suspicious and mean. A bunch of them had recently killed two young VISTA workers by tying the 20-year-old women from prestigious Northeastern universities up in their cars and strangling them with piano wire.

My brother had driven a girl home from Burger King one night after their shift—an honest-to-god nice thing to do by a good guy—and her father met them in the driveway with a shotgun, snarling and threatening Paul with death if he ever showed up again.

*

"What'd you do?" I pleaded with Doug during his single phone call. The answer was just so Doug: "I was taking a dump behind the car ..."

"Oh, man, Doug, you had a date," I said, pleading.

"... and this cruiser pulls up, turns on its lights and the guy hauls me in for drunk driving. I was drunk shitting when he caught me, but I wasn't driving. Man, I really had to go. Dad-blamed Nazi pig."

A couple of months hence, Doug called at about 3 a.m.—2 a.m. Central time—on a Sunday from New Orleans. He asked if I'd come and get him. I said, "Sure." New Orleans is about a 20-hour drive. When he got home a couple of days later, he had forgotten the phone call.

*

The drunken wrecks began to mount up after a few years. I lost count at around 10, some of which were actually serious. I hit a bridge near Statesville, N.C. once and when the cop arrived, he asked if I'd been drinking and I said, "Oh, no, officer" even as he surveyed a 30-yard-long string of Miller cans snaking behind the injured yellow pickup. Different cop, different time, different place (Blue Ridge Parkway near Roanoke), same scenario: I'd rolled three times, blood covered my T-shirt, my breath smelled like St. Paddy's Day, and the Toyota was a crushed shell, surrounded by Old Milwaukee cans. I'd changed brands somewhere along the way. This time I broke my nose on an open ash tray. It was one of three breaks. Two wives broke it with unexpected roundhouse punches before and after the wreck. I had the capacity to make the Pope lose his temper when I was drinking.

I had a post-midnight, Thanksgiving Day wreck in Asheville's Kenilworth neighborhood, where I lived, in about 1968. There, a block from my log cabin, sat my proudest possession, a black, 1965 Olds 442 with white leather interior. It was in this lady's yard, the morning after—I'd stolen off in the night while the 442 was still steaming from the wreck, ran home and hid 'till dawn. The 442 was sitting stark and injured on the back side of a tree. Its right front fender was crushed and there was a severe scar on a mature pin oak, sharply to the lower right, a position that, when matched with the crushed fender would have been impossible to achieve, coming off the sharp curve, as I obviously had.

The loss of the car, the cop trying intently to pin something on me in the glare of the morning light, the furious old lady, hands on hips, staring at her plowed flower bed; none of it had the effect of the wonder at the physics of the thing. How do you hit right-on-right, slip by on the left (the tracks in the lady's previously manicured yard said so) and wind up facing the tree on the other side?

*

Of course, there's the legendary tale of a famous Southern Writer and the three-day drunk, which I'm told I was involved in as a driver, but don't much remember. This was during my brief stint as a student at UNC Asheville (Asheville-Biltmore College at the time) when I was asked to pick up the late Southern poet laureate and writer of a hot bestseller at the Asheville airport near Hendersonville. Dickey saw me, recognized the youthful awe and said, "Where's a man get a drink in this town?" He didn't say "one-horse town," but that's what he meant. We didn't make it back to school. I was his driver and drinking buddy for those three days and put him back on a plane at the end. My English teacher was not amused.

*

The AA stories I hear to this day of the afflicted are filled with joy and wonder, a kind of embarrassed exhilaration that nobody was killed—when that's the case—and the mountain climber's rush of having conquered. But it is most often short-lived and self-deprecating. And humiliating and painful and nauseating and disgusting and, oh, so sad.

There was the old man, new to the program, bemoaning that the officer who'd arrested him, and was ultimately responsible for his mandatory AA attendance, was "a *girl*, and a dad-gum *dog catcher*! Gaa-hhhhhd Dang! I ain't never been that embarrassed...."

Longtime sober Trish describes how on a late-night bender, she'd torn away from the party to make a beer run to a 7-11 a mile away. Her daughter was killed instantly in the wreck and Trish didn't get a scratch. She doesn't cry when she talks about it now. She's cried out and she understands her story and her daughter's sacrifice have probably saved dozens of little girls from being similarly snuffed.

There's one sober story that makes me smile every time I think of it, probably a smug smile. I was driving back from a Big South Conference tournament semifinal basketball game in Lynchburg where UNC Asheville had frittered away a big lead and lost a game it should have won. I saw this blue light in my rearview. I pulled over and a young cop ambled up and asked for my driver's license.

"Do you know why I stopped you?" she asked, a question with a big trap in the middle.

"Not for drunk driving," I said, smiling.

"What?" she said.

"Never mind. No, ma'am, I don't know."

*

I'm told that every half-hour in this country somebody is killed by a drunk driver and that every 30 seconds somebody is similarly hurt. Sixty percent of us have wrecks while drinking at some point and, yeah, almost all of us have mixed alcohol and driving illegally. It's not pretty.

GETTIN' SOBER

The whiskey that once settled the dust
And tasted so fine now tastes so faint
And the memories that once floated out come back stronger
More clearly with each drink you take
"Slow Movin' Outlaw," Waylon Jennings

That was one of those country music classics that kept me entertained through years of a kind of sickness that seemed to have no end. During the last few years of my partnership with the bottle, a time when I couldn't get high any longer, only leaden and depressed, I wanted to change that second line of Waylon's song to read "And tasted so fine now tastes of pain." That's what it had become.

Drinking was involuntary, like a sneeze. Stopping didn't appear to be an option. Until one day when I simply decided it was time, as I had with cigarettes. People in recovery say it's becoming "sick and tired of being sick and tired" and it's a powerful motivator.

*

AA had begun for me in 1972 following my second DUI (the first coming about 18 months earlier on my wedding night) when Judge James Brice, in effect, sentenced me to AA instead of the can, giving me the choice. I think of this as the Neolithic Period of the program, which was founded by a Toledo stockbroker and a physician in 1939. The book *Alcoholics Anonymous* (commonly called The Big Book), which they wrote, strongly reflects the fact that they were in trades other than writing.

AA had grown in numbers a great deal, but was basically what it started out as: an organization of middle-aged-to-old white male drunks who smoked, drank coffee, cussed about everything and had a monumental group grump that I only later learned was not required in the literature.

Most at the church basement meeting I regularly attended were war veterans and wanted to be John Wayne or at least Audie Murphy—strong, silent, brooding. Many didn't shave more than once a week, just enough to let you know they knew how, but didn't care. One or two occasionally dressed in business casual, but the majority worked in one capacity or another for The Railroad—Roanoke's major employer at the time. They weren't educated, didn't speak well and I didn't think they were especially sharp.

But they'd tell you, "Boy, if you keep coming to meetings and do what we tell you, you'll be just like us." And they'd smile as if that were a desirable thing.

There was one old boy whose name has long since escaped me, who was said to have fought in every American conflict of the 20th Century, starting with the Philippine Insurrection in 1913, as that conflict for the islands' independence wound down. He'd been in every branch of service and even fought as a mercenary when there were no official wars to join. He never said much, but was always the first at the meeting and the last to leave, spending a lot of the time between those events sitting on a deep couch and nodding off. I guess he was tired.

I didn't last in this atmosphere—though I did put in a year of Sundays—thinking I was much too smart, much too handsome, much too sophisticated for these fools, and eventually determined that drinking had more to offer than this kind of sobriety.

I made a few more fumbling attempts over the next 22 years when the misery index topped out, realizing there was a pretty severe problem, but thinking that the cure was worse than the disease.

When I finally got back to AA for real, it had changed dramatically: half the members were women, many were young (including teenagers), meetings were brisk and upbeat, people dressed better and combed their hair. They seemed better educated and better able to convey how all this worked. It seemed to fit better, to be less of a punishment and more of a treatment. In the Roanoke Valley, the program had grown from a few scattered meetings each week to more than 100.

Still, I didn't have a clue how to do this, and that became more obvious as time went on.

*

The first rule of getting sober—after "don't drink, and go to meetings"— is, "Don't get involved with a member of the opposite sex (same sex if you're gay) for a year. More if you can hold out."

So, five minutes into sobriety, I met this Brenda, an interesting personality, a spinner and weaver, working on a degree in mythology and storytelling at Hollins University. She was from an old Botetourt County family with Civil War ties and slave holdings in the old days. She had an easy smile, curled at the corners, slightly crooked eye teeth, a genuine twinkle in gray-green eyes, with a bit of the witch—good witch, I thought—looking out from under all that latte-colored hair. She was a "Jungian with overtones of Campbell," meaning Joseph Campbell, who was trendy at the time.

She was depressive and bulimic, both of which took me a while to determine. I didn't find out about the bulimia for about nine months or so, until a friend asked me if I knew and I said, "Know what?"

"She's bulimic."

"What's that?"

"You know, binge and purge. Eat until you can't fit another pint of ice cream in; stick your finger down your throat; eat some more; repeat finger maneuver."

"Sounds smart," I said. "It keeps her pretty small, I'd say, without all that diet and exercise crap."

"Yeah, and pretty sick. That's why her teeth are gray. The vomit stains them. Didn't you ever notice? It's obsessive-compulsive behavior, not unlike your own disease."

Nope, I hadn't noticed. I knew she had a lot of dental bills, but frankly, I was so self-absorbed with this sobriety deal, that it was remarkable I remembered her name or much else about her.

We moved into the same house with a couple of her cats who sat wrapped around her as she read, a near constant state of affairs, but it was a ghostly relationship and when she started making sounds like my mother when Mom was depressed, I withdrew quickly and thoroughly. It reached the point where if she touched me, it hurt—real, physical hurt.

So we split and my brother, Sandy, when he found out, said, "Hey, when you hook up with the next one, see if you can get one that shaves her legs." That reminded me of the advice Mom gave me when I divorced one of my middle wives: "Would you *please* marry a dumb one?"

I didn't know quite how to handle either of those recommendations, so I hooked up with a tall, gangly, intense woman in AA. Her first and last names rhyme and I can't tell you what they are because of the anonymity promise in AA, but think Kitty Wells married to Conway Twitty and you get a general idea.

Mistake II, The Movie. Not even fully a year in AA yet. Old habits die harder than Bruce Willis.

Yet another mood swing queen who was utterly charming, bright and fascinating one minute and doing Linda Blair with the pea soup the next. She came equipped with this thoroughly troubled, intrusive teen-aged son who could pitch a pout through a tire at 50 yards without ever touching the Goodyear on the side. That kid could manipulate and you could see, without much effort, where he learned it.

Neither she nor I had a year of sobriety and we looked like actors in a soap opera. That was bound to score big points. The breakup, contrary to what seemed to be coming, was more a whimper than a screaming hissy-fit and I couldn't have been more pleased.

I came away from those two missteps a bit wiser, and with a love of books from Brenda and jazz from Miss Rhyming Names. Thank you, ma'ams.

I was Oh (or Ow!) for Two and hanging on to my dry-drunk sobriety with fingernails chewed to the knuckle. Then it came to me in a late afternoon Tuesday AA meeting like the voice of God: "Don't get involved for a year."

Oh. That.

My late sponsor Tom Shirley, a college professor who was funny and wise and knew women about as well as any man I've ever known—and boy, did he love 'em—once told me that if I went to enough meetings, I'd soak up a lot of the wisdom in them through my pores, through osmosis.

If I'd stay away from women for a few minutes, my chances would improve dramatically, he instructed.

I went to 200 meetings in six months. That takes the standard recommendation of 90 meetings in 90 days—for mental and emotional cleansing and reorientation—and more than doubles it. No women, just meetings, sometimes three in a day. And, no, I had to repeat, three meetings, not three women. I had gone to my first AA meeting 22 years earlier and still hadn't picked up a one-month chip, so I figured the least I could do was show up.

Smartest thing I ever did.

*

Meetings can often take on tones variously of standup comedy, gut-wrenching shrink sessions, consultations with Indian mystics, shamelessly mixed metaphors, greeting card sappiness, religious interpretation for agnostics, or simply a discussion of baffling or joyful events.

For a couple of years, I put together a newsletter for the Roanoke Valley Intergroup, the closest AA comes to organization, in which I compiled a column called "Heard at AA." These were a compilation of real quotes from meetings I attended.

Examples:

• "I'm not much, but I'm all I ever think about."
• "I sold my house rather than deal with [visitors]. I couldn't just say, 'Don't come over.'"
• "If you're in early recovery and things are going smoothly, you're delusional."
• "Alcoholics don't fall in love, they take hostages."
• "Dogs give unconditional love. Cats give unconditional indifference."
• "God did not stamp 'critic' on my behind."
• "I've cried so much in recent years … I can watch a Hallmark card commercial and damn near have to go to the psych center."
• "Moderation would be what? One or two blackouts a day?"
• "If you drink in moderation, maybe your problems will come in moderation. Maybe you'll only shoot somebody once."
• "God gave us spirituality and the devil organized it into religion."
• "I was doing objective manifestations of how I was growing down."

- "If you can stay sober in AA, you can stay sober anywhere."
- "We don't kick crazy people out."
- "I don't have a clue, but that never stopped me before."
- "It was really unusual Friday. I walked out of two meetings."
- "AA is Christianity for dyslexics."
- "I'm not self-centered. I've been getting drunk since I was a teenager for the benefit of mankind."
- Alcoholism "is not some minor inconvenience."
- "He was a teabag Christian. He only prayed when he was in hot water."
- "I find some amazing things in those quiet places. I go back into my quiet space and find serenity."
- "Don't worry about God. Just get into the habit of prayer."
- "The bungee cord of this program has to snap me back every 72 hours or I don't have serenity."
- "I was raised in that breeding ground for alcoholics: the Good Christian Home."
- "I didn't come to AA because it was a bad TV night."
- "Faith isn't faith until it's all you have."
- "This is one of those amazing meetings where everything fits like a lightning bolt."
- [Two AAs in chance meeting in a grocery store line: "Good to see you. I'd better go get in this [longer] line so I can work on my patience."
- "Picking relationships is like getting a good deal at Goodwill: Great price; it's broke, *but I can take it home and fix it.*"
- "I felt like an elephant on roller skates."
- "I'm glad my sponsor's not a kangaroo. I get to ride in her *back* pocket and see where she's been."
- "What works for me is redundancy."
- "My wife doesn't get on me nearly as much when I get on my knees to pray as she did when I used to get on my knees to puke."
- "I need a cranial rectonomy—the act of extricating one's head from one's ass."
- "That's when I click the bitch switch."
  *

There are a few common basic fears among newly recovering alcoholics—and, I'd imagine, people trying to get over anything that has dominated their lives to this degree for a spell:

"What will I do with my spare time? Will I be bored? Will I be boring? How do I avoid that?"

Tough questions from people who haven't been anything but bored and boring for all of their recent years.

Those questions covered me like Gramdma Smith's smelly old quilt, the one infested with bedbugs. Boredom and anxiety still showed up on a regular basis, but my med-cin wasn't around.

The new cure? Work out. Eat sweets. Take Vitamin B and C. Call people in AA and talk. My pal Sylvia gave me an involved explanation about how the body's chemical processes are out of balance when we drink heavily and it takes a while to get them back in line. Vitamin C is gone and needs to be replaced. Vitamin D quells the urge to drink. Sweets meet the urge for an immediate fix. Working out triggers the endorphins, pretty much the same high I got with beer, but without the hangover.

Most alcoholics—80 percent, I've read—have the added burden of being clinically depressed while they're making major physical and emotional changes in their lives. There was every indication that I should have been in that 80 percent, since Mom was an early poster child for depression, but I only got Dad's disease and as I watched those poor souls suffering with both diseases at once, I felt fortunate to only be a drunk.

My friend Rod, who had the dual diagnosis, talked about his "dark place," which always brought to mind the lyric to an old Eddie Raven song about a guy fighting depression and alcoholism: "I ain't dancin' with those demons/I ain't dealin' with that devil any more." Rod railed at AA's narrow focus on chemical dependency without addressing the need for treatment of depression with counseling and a drug cocktail of some description. I could see his point. The counseling was supplementary and the drugs had improved to the point that they simply leveled moods, erasing the extremes. Some of them also whacked hell out of your sexuality, but Mom had been treated with borderline-barbaric electrical shock therapy only 25 years earlier.

Improvement for me was gradual, but obvious. In meetings, we talked about the "little daily miracles" and I slowly began buying in to what I was hearing. There was the religious element—or at least what I perceived to be a religious element—that came clear one evening when I heard this small woman named Pat, a hotel maid, I think, talk about accepting a higher power, one of the elements in AA's structure that is difficult for people who've lived lives on or near the bottom with the perception that they've been abandoned by the God of other people's understanding.

Even during the drinking years (here, 1981) I cared about the kids, though I was never much of a father

Pat said, "I just couldn't get it. Then one night, as a meeting finished and everybody got up from the table, I saw all these Styrofoam coffee cups sitting on the table. I went around and collected all of them I could and took them home. They were my higher power—a reminder of everybody in the room—until what I believe now came along."

Tom told me to "stop trying to figure it out. Just pray. It doesn't matter who to. Do it until you get it, and you'll get it."

"But how do you do it? I mean, really: how?"

Tom looked at me for a minute, knowingly. He'd been here before: "The 11th Step says to pray 'only for knowledge of His will for us and the power to carry that out.' Pretty simple. Show me what to do and give me sense enough to do it."

And, yeah. It worked. Worked quickly and thoroughly. I was not given a physical rendition of this Higher Power thing, but I got a place to go when I was confused, when I was celebrating, when I had a question. I lost that gnawing, diverting, consuming exigency for a drink. It simply wasn't there one day and it hasn't come back.

"It's all inside," Tom kept saying, and I was starting to see where "inside" was situated in the scheme of this new way of viewing life.

*

Practical considerations stared at me immediately after I picked up that white chip in front of about 100 AA people, many of whom knew me and my history, in 1994. My publisher knew I drank heavily, but it didn't seem to be a major concern to him. I decided to tell him I was going to AA anyway, because he deserved to know. A colleague of mine, working at the newspaper in Martinsville a few years earlier, had been a practicing alcoholic for years, but he got to work and did his job without any major catastrophes. When he told his managing editor he was going to AA and hadn't had a drink in a couple of months, he was fired. Later, he killed himself. So, I was probably taking a chance.

Jim Lindsey had bought the paper from Andrew Horne and he and I worked well together, if the printed product is the only consideration. There was a good bit of friction getting to that point, though. A psychologist Jim hired to evaluate our working relationship determined that I tended to work in a manner that employed the strategy, "Ready, fire, aim." Jim's approach was, "Ready, aim, aim, aim, aim…." And, frankly, we drove each other nuts. I wanted to plough ahead; Jim was pulling back the reins with both hands, screaming, "Don't do anything until I get there," then not showing up for days at a time. He liked to work, sweat, argue and grow his beard all night on deadline. I wanted everything done two weeks early, efficiently and neatly—between 9 a.m. and 5 p.m.

Early in our relationship, we went together to Danville every month to take the pasted-down newspaper flats and have the Journal printed at McCain Printing. We had hired the staff at the Bedford Bulletin to set the type and paste it to the newspaper-sized card stock so the printer could photograph it, make plates and run the press. Jim was never satisfied with the way the flats looked and he fiddled with "straightening" straight type for hours while the press guys waited for the pages in Danville. It drove me nuts and I finally refused to go to Danville with him any more.

But, I think we were good for each other ultimately, me learning detail work, persistence, and the question, "How does that work?" and he discovering that if you don't do things, things don't get done.

When I told Jim of my AA commitment, he said, frankly and without reservation, "Do what you have to do. I'm behind you completely. You don't need to explain or apologize." I don't think I'll ever forget that. It was one of the most unselfish moments I've ever lived through and it was aimed at me.

What Jim's "permission" allowed were noon and late afternoon meetings when I needed them—every day for a while—breaking from work when I wanted to talk to a sponsor, and a period of healing that pressure at work could have endangered.

I had quit my 3 ½ packs a day cigarette habit a year before, so that didn't enter the recovery equation, but diet did. My diet, as a drinker, was awful. Ultimately, I ate only when I had to because eating interfered with drinking and smoking killed my appetite, in any case. After I quit smoking, I ate more, which made the alcohol react differently and it all just screwed up my enjoyment of eating, smoking, drinking, anything. I gained weight, as well. At the same time I had quit smoking the year before—the same day, I think—my metabolism slowed down and I gained about 30 pounds quickly.

Dental care had gone in the toilet over the years and my teeth were starting to warn me that they were going to fall out if I didn't do something. I discovered that dental health is one of the huge challenges recovering people face. Fortunately, I had good insurance and after I married Christina, she made certain that I faced the fear of the dental community and got my teeth fixed.

I had some other physical problems, notably erectile dysfunction—"limp weenie syndrome" is the medical term, according to Tom—common among alcoholics and smokers, I learned, but I wasn't in the kind of desperate condition I saw so many others enduring. So many drunks get healthy just in time to enjoy dying of all the awful things they did to themselves. I was in pretty good shape, all things considered.

The conventional wisdom in AA is that you have to change everything about yourself as quickly as you can in order to begin recovering. It's a tall order, especially when you have friends and family, hobbies, habits, routines. It can be daunting, but Tom said, "Don't try to do everything at once. Just go to meetings. Go to as many as you can. What you don't get by listening and understanding, you'll get by osmosis."

It was in the meetings that I developed new friendships and that harmful potential was left outside. They offered both an escape and an alternative. I liked these people. They were smart and many of them were accomplished. They spoke well, thought thoroughly and came to conclusions that had escaped me for 45 years, healthy conclusions that were appealing.

These better habits, better friends, better circumstances, better attitudes began to accumulate and as they did, life as I knew it disappeared, replaced with something I had never dreamed of—or even wanted—when I was still drinking. My whole goal when I finally gave up was having some say in what was happening to me. I wanted to be able to avoid drinking when I didn't want to drink, which was most of the time, and I wanted to be able to get up in the morning and look back on the previous evening without embarrassment or dread about what I might have done.

I began to awake feeling invigorated, ready for work, ready to see people, ready to experiment, to be entertained.

While I was drinking I was always "working on a book," which was utter bullshit. An awful lot of writers tell that tale at some time during their lives, covering for having done little with their "God-given talent," which is really more of a craft, except in the hands of an artist. I believed I was working on a book, even though I didn't have a printed line to show anybody. I did think about it.

After I got sober, I produced two books in 18 months. It was easy. I won awards for my work and I felt respected. I was asked to be on boards of directors, to take part in the community. People I respect started calling me a "community leader," which made me laugh. "Hell, if they'll follow a drunk, they'll follow a fool," I thought. George Bush II was elected president a few years later.

*

AA has some problems and I have had some problems with it over the years, but my experience is that if you're a drunk and you do what the people in AA tell you to do, you'll get sober. I think that was too simple a message for a long time.

I'm the distinguished gentleman in the center with the mustache,
flanked by members of the Roanoke Times and Roanoke World-News
sports staffs, covering a high school basketball all-star game in 1976

PART VI:
THE END

—30—

The first part of this book—everything before this chapter—was written in a month. I've always written fast and generally finished pieces in one take. But I ran out of things to say before I got to the end and so I went looking for advice.

My friend Betsy Gehman, who's in her 80s and has lived a life we'd all like a crack at, said, "You're not dead. Why end the book?"

Good point.

"Well, Betsy, what about the later years, the ones I've been living since I met you and Christina [my last—I hope— and best wife] and got sober and made peace with a lot of people and joined the natural order?" I asked.

"This is not a book about being normal," she said. "It's a book about you."

Well, yeah. That would be it.

Normal, the way I have been for some years now, was not the way I spent my first 50 years or so. As you've seen, there was a lot of conflict and turbulence, a lot of false starts and serious mistakes, confusion and pain, resistance and emotional combat. Some of it was pretty funny.

When my great and good friend Sue L. directed me towards the front door of AA in one of those inexplicable life moments that you simply can't predict or anticipate, all I knew changed. I was afraid of that change, terrified of it, especially at first when I wondered what I would do with myself, how sober people had fun. As if drunk people knew something about it.

There's been this quiet contentment, slowing down my body and my mind and looking at what is around me. Christina would not have taken a second look at me two years before we met, but we are marvelously matched at this point in our lives. My family has joined just about everybody else I know in telling me I "married up," a distinctly mixed message when one is on the receiving end of that assessment.

My kids have settled into comfortable patterns (Evan has a daughter, Madeline, for whom this book was originally intended) and for that I'm grateful because they have the genes and the training to make my mistakes, to be crazy. They're smarter, though, I think.

I like my life as it is winding down, mellowing out, reaching goals, finding its level. I've accomplished more in real terms in the last few years than I did in the first 50, but I wouldn't trade that first 50, even with all the pain it absorbed. It's what made the most recent years so rich for me. I once said I'd trade all the pain in the world for 10 minutes of being in love with Kathryn Rhoads and, by God, the Mother of All Things took me up on that and left me wondering at the sanity of the swap. But I think I was right. Happiness is expensive. Lessons are expensive. Life is expensive.

If this is a bit on the drippy sentimental side and out of character for me, it's about the only way I can finish my story. I don't know how it will end ultimately, but at this point, I suppose I could say we lived happily ever after, at least until today. That's all I'll bet on, anyway.

Grandpa with Evan's daughter, Madeline, watching a University of Tennessee football game. This one's for you, kid. Go Vols!

Oh, One More Thing

When I was in my senior year of high school in Avery County, living at Grandfather Home for Children, there was an old farm hand named Grover, who took care of the home's livestock, which included some big old hogs. One day I was down at the pen and Grover said, "Wanna see somethin' funny?" and I said, "Sure." He bent over, picked up this three-foot-long stick, reached through the rail fence and started rubbing a 300-pound sow on the belly with it. The sow didn't resist, didn't flinch, didn't look at Grover, grinning like a relative. She just flopped over on her side and went straight-away asleep. "They'll do that ever time," the old man said.

I took Grover's stick and rubbed it on another hog. Scraaaaatch. Flop, snooooooooze.

Printed in the United States
88423LV00005B/184-198/A